# INVESTING IN
# INTANGIBLE ASSETS

# INVESTING IN INTANGIBLE ASSETS

*Finding and Profiting From
Hidden Corporate Value*

**RUSSELL L. PARR**

**JOHN WILEY & SONS, INC.**

New York / Chichester / Brisbane / Toronto / Singapore

This publication is designed to provide accurate and authoritative information in regard to the subject matter covered. It is sold with the understanding that the publisher is not engaged in rendering legal, accounting, or other professional service. If legal advice or other expert assistance is required, the services of a competent professional person should be sought. *From a Declaration of Principles jointly adopted by a Committee of the American Bar Association and a Committee of Publishers.*

The names of all products to which reference is made herein may be protected by federal, state, or common-law trademark laws and may be trademarks or registered trademarks of their respective companies. All terms thought to be trademarks are appropriately capitalized throughout this book.

*Library of Congress Cataloging in Publication Data:*

Parr, Russell L.
    Investing in intangible assets : finding and profiting from hidden corporate value / Russell L. Parr.
        p.   cm.
    Includes bibliographical references.
    ISBN 0-471-53038-7 (cloth)
    1. Investments.   2. Intangible property.   3. Corporations-
-Valuation.   I. Title
HG4521.P355   1991
658.15′2—dc20
                                                        90-23442
                                                           CIP

Printed in the United States of America

10  9  8  7  6  5  4  3  2  1

This book and all of my love is
for Jane.

Always and Forever, Darling.

# PREFACE

Intangible asset investing is the fundamental business trend for the 1990s. Proprietary intangible assets like patents and trademarks capture markets, command premium pricing, and support huge manufacturing efficiencies. These assets are the source of earnings, growth, and investment success. They present competitors with formidable economic barriers and represent the foundation of corporate value. In some cases, these assets can even cushion the impact of economic recessions.

Serious investors must turn their attention to the power of these hidden assets to fully understand the foundation of winning stocks. This book tries to fill the rather large gap that exists between understanding the financial performance of a company and understanding the nature of the hidden intangible assets that are the source of earnings and ultimately corporate value.

Evidence of this trend can be found by looking at mergers and acquisitions. Corporations are acquiring intangible assets all the time. Real estate and oil reserves were once the driving force behind corporate takeovers. Now the coveted crown jewels of corporate takeovers are patents, trademarks, copyrights, and distribution networks.

Corporations are also creating intangible assets. Philip Morris spent over $2 billion last year just to support and maintain its portfolio of trademarks and Procter & Gamble spent $1 billion. Research budgets also approach stratospheric levels with over $55.5 billion spent in 1987 by industry aimed at creating new technologies and monopolistic patents. Intangible assets are part of almost every growing and valuable company, yet too little attention is focused on this vital aspect of stock investing.

Famous trade names and patented technology are examples of intangible assets but only scratch the surface. This book focuses on the fundamental importance of many different types of intangible assets and reveals the hidden ways in which these assets drive stock values.

Successful investing cannot be accomplished in the current environment without a full understanding of the unique characteristics of this diverse and complex group of hidden assets. This book is the first to address intangible assets from this important and fresh investment perspective. When coupled with traditional fundamental analysis, the insights in this book will help investors to translate the power of hidden intangible assets into winning stock selections.

By reading *Investing in Intangible Assets,* investors will come to see the importance of analyzing companies from an intangible asset perspective. They will also learn to be careful because they will learn that the power and potential of many intangible assets are fragile. Careful analysis is required and this book focuses on the important areas of intangible asset strengths and weaknesses.

Professional, institutional, and individual investors should find the unique concepts in this book compelling. More specifically, the primary audience includes individual investors, stockbrokers, security analysts, investment bankers, portfolio mangers, and financial planners. Also, lawyers, patent attorneys, trademark attorneys, and accountants will enjoy the different approach for assessing stock values which is presented.

This book shows the following:

1.  Intangible assets are the foundation of corporate value and should be the primary focus of investment decisions in the 1990s.

2. Accounting statements are not at all complete with regard to intangibles and investors must learn where to look to gain the information that is needed to fill the gaps.

3. Intangible assets extend far beyond patents and trademarks and include items that are not easily recognized but are equally important.

4. Intangible assets such as patents and trademarks require continuous care and feeding. When this is missing, stock values drop.

5. Many intangibles have definite lives. A track record of earnings growth may not be sustainable. Investment values can vanish if certain steps are not taken. Investors will learn what to look for in judging this aspect of intangible assets.

6. There are many alternative avenues for deriving value from the ownership of intangible assets. High stock values are awarded to companies that fully exploit their intangible assets.

7. Wall Street takeovers are currently driven by the quest to obtain intangible assets.

8. A company that does not possess intangible assets is not likely ever to be very valuable.

9. Earnings may be the foundation of value but intangibles are the source of earnings.

10. Different intangible assets contribute to value in different ways. These variations can affect stock values significantly.

Smokestacks and industrial facilities are no longer a vital part of corporate or investment success. Investors must now learn to conceptualize stock investments in light of the new and powerful intangible assets that have come to dominate and drive corporate success. The investment strategy for the 1990s is to invest in solid companies that have intangible assets that are fully exploited.

Russell L. Parr
East Brunswick, New Jersey

January 1991

# ACKNOWLEDGMENTS

Many individuals contribute to the creation of a book. Most often, long lists of professional colleagues and inspirational educators are lauded for their herculean hours of counseling, review, and comment. Nothing of the kind will intrude on these pages. Instead, my most sincere gratitude is offered to the most important contributors—my family and friends. These are the people who have had the greatest effect on my professional and personal lives. They have contributed to this book in many ways. They have encouraged me to strive a little bit harder to make them a little bit prouder.

Henry Melvin Parr lovingly spent countless hours providing boundless encouragement, instruction, and attention mixed with reinforcing praise. He instilled the confidence that has served me in all my business and personal endeavors, culminating in the nerve to write this, rather good, book. My father handed down a tradition of honest principles on which to build a life. He never finished his book but unknowingly inspired this one.

Dorothy Ann Parr has contributed to my life and this book by providing the safest of safe havens from which to test new waters. She has always provided unwavering encouragement, support, and love. New projects always carry the risk of failure but my mother has always provided a safety net of warm hugs that have allowed me to attempt new heights and ever more complicated tricks. Thanks Mom.

Richard Scott Parr brought to this book fresh insights about business, patent law, pharmaceuticals, economics, and life. He is a treasure trove of interesting ideas and information. My brother has an easy-going exterior nature that belies his limitless energy for new ideas. For him, everything is possible. His example has propelled me through the slow moments that frustrate every writer. His acceptance of my different investment views gave me confidence to present daring concepts. My brother is quite a fellow indeed.

Kathleen Parr Kobran is my very artistic and sensitive sister. Her many prestigious accomplishments in serious vocal orchestrations have provided a balance to my life. Her example proves that great success can be achieved outside the world of commerce. Subtle balances that sneak into parts of this book are derived from Kit.

Alicia Parr always brings bubbling enthusiasm to every family event. She has a "can do" attitude that left a fresh breeze in some of these pages where stale first drafts once stood. Allied with my brother Richard, she will undoubtedly inspire me to attempt even bolder projects in the future.

Alan Kobran provided front line entrepreneurial insight for many of the topics in this book. He has always shared with me his exciting venture capital experiences from which I have gained an insider's understanding about the exhaustive efforts required to give birth to new innovations.

Before a word hits the page there is a lot of talking. Endless rambling can often establish outlines and themes. Sometimes the rambling is incoherent. Only true friends would endure such haranguing and then happily make plans to meet for dinner again next week. Don Palombi, Mike Brill, and Cliff Herrington are my best friends. They have allowed me to boast about my grand triumphs while helping to soothe the wounded pride of failures. They know all about me and like me anyway.

Some of my best ideas, the kind that come in a flash and then endure the tests of analytical investigation, have been inspired by quiet moments at the bar with Gordon V. Smith. He thinks that he is my boss and colleague but he is really my dear friend.

Late at night, severe doubts can establish rather strong positions. Advancing ideas can be stopped cold. At those times, gentle voices repeatedly said "Don't worry, its going to be great." The sincere enthusiasm and blind faith that have steadfastly been provided by Jeff Brown and Marla Bobowick of John Wiley & Sons are greatly appreciated.

Thanks Everyone.

# CONTENTS

# INVESTING IN
# INTANGIBLE ASSETS

# 1

# INTRODUCTION: The Future Is Intangible

Walt Disney Company attempted an acquisition last year costing an estimated $200 million. Manufacturing facilities, real estate, and financial securities were all *absent* from the transaction. The investment was completely intangible. Targeted were the Muppet characters—Kermit the Frog, Miss Piggy, and the rest of the gang. The plan was for the company to gather a whole host of new characters to use in its operations all over the world. As part of the acquisition the company would have obtained nearly 300 television series episodes and five feature films. Jeffrey Katzenburg, president of Walt Disney Studios, was quoted in *The Wall Street Journal* about the longevity of the investment, saying, "And they're all evergreen—you're dealing with material that does not age."

Intangible assets are the new frontier of successful investing. Understanding the nature of these assets and their contribution to earnings is now vital for selecting companies in which to invest. Intangible assets are at the heart of successful companies. These hidden assets include intellectual property such as keystone patents and well established trademarks. Also in this category are copyrights, distribution networks, and, for some companies like Disney, cartoon characters.

Patents, trademarks, and other intangible assets are becoming the main focus of business activity with emphasis on optimum exploitation. Corporations that properly create, acquire, and manage these vital assets will be in commanding positions of economic power.

In *Microcosm: The Quantum Revolution in Economics and Technology,* George Gilder explains that wealth is no longer derived from possessing physical resources. "Wealth and power came mainly to the possessor of material things or to the ruler of military forces capable of conquering the physical means of production: land, labor, and capital." Gilder explains that "today, the ascendant nations and corporations are masters not of land and material resources but of ideas and technologies."

Intangible assets such as patents and trademarks are the legal embodiment of some of the ideas and technology to which Gilder is referring.

The mere possession of industrial capacity or raw materials is not enough to assure continued growth and profitability. The use of steel, coal, oil, and other resources as part of our gross national product is shrinking. For example, only 2% of the cost of a silicon chip is represented by raw materials. Lacking unique intangible assets, all that remains for a corporation is the ability to mass produce a commodity or to manufacture for others as a job-shop. Either fate usually means slow growth, slim profits, and poor stock performance. Only a proprietary technological advantage, well regarded trademark, or other proprietary intangible asset can save a corporate investment from mediocrity.

The transformation of Eastern Europe into capitalistic economies will initially provide developed countries with new sources of inexpensive manufacturing capabilities. In the 1990s, countries like

---

Key Investment Concept # 1

The business world is splitting in two: those that have intangible assets and those that do not. The "have nots" will fade away unless they can gain access to intangibles like patented technology and well regarded trademarks.

---

Rumania, Czechoslovakia, Hungary, East Germany, and Bulgaria will play the role that Japan and South Korea filled in the 1960s. Companies that possess intangible assets will be able to prosper from this situation while job-shops and commodity manufacturers will find themselves besieged by new pressures from abroad: new pressures that weren't even considered possible only a few years ago.

## Intangible Asset Contributions

Unfortunately, investors that look at earnings, cash flow, and market potential neglect to focus on the vital intangible assets that are the driving force of earnings and company value. Almost everyone agrees that high profits, solid return on investment, and accelerated growth are important characteristics for successful stock investments. Very few, however, bother to identify and analyze the intangible assets that drive revenues, profits, and growth. Yet these are the most important assets that a company can possess.

Above-average earnings come from well managed intangible assets. They contribute by saving in production costs or by extracting a premium price in the market. In the end, the overall profitability for a company that has valuable intangible assets is usually above average.

Patented technology can contribute to earnings by saving the production inputs of labor or materials. By passing along a portion of these savings to customers, market share gains can be achieved while profitability is simultaneously enhanced.

Intangible assets can also contribute directly at the retail level by commanding premium prices for otherwise ordinary merchandise. Trademarks provide the best example. At almost any department store a large assortment of polo shirts can be found. Material quality and construction are often equal yet price tags can easily vary by as much as $40. An unbranded, all cotton polo shirt can be had for $25. When the Ralph Lauren logo is placed on the breast pocket the same shirt sells for $65. As long as the entire premium price isn't spent on trademark advertising support, and it rarely happens, then a significant amount of the premium goes to bottom line profitability. The premium exists because of an intangible asset.

At another level, an intangible advantage can be possession of an enormous distribution network, which provides access to important wholesalers. Investors in start-up companies that are fascinated by a hot product better look at how the product is going to get to market. Without a distribution network and access to retail channels, hot products can turn very cold in the warehouse. With a distribution system, a company not only moves the goods but can often own a formidable barrier to competition, as is discussed later in Chapter 3.

In Chapter 4, a financial analysis of specialty chemicals companies will show that technological intangible assets are responsible for superior company profits. When technological intangible assets are absent, profit levels are low or at deficit levels. The specialty chemicals industry was used only as an example. Superior profits can be found across many industries when technological intangible assets are present.

## Acquisitions and Takeovers Focus on Intangible Assets Coveted Crown Jewels

Deal makers and corporate raiders are just starting to focus on intangible assets. Chapter 2 shows that the most recent acquisitions around the world focus on intangibles. Undervalued assets used to be excess cash, oil reserves, and appreciated real estate. Now the assets with the greatest potential for enhanced exploitation are intangible.

General Electric bought RCA for its space technology. Grand Metropolitan ( U.K. conglomerate) was attracted to the trademarks possessed by Pillsbury. Philip Morris purchased Kraft, Inc. and acquired one of the best collections of consumer product brand names in the United States. Maxwell Communications purchased Mac-

---

**Key Investment Concept # 2**

Intangible assets have become the coveted crown jewels of takeover artists.

---

millan, Inc. and received an irreplaceable collection of active book titles.

Some of the most popular takeover targets are the owners of well known trademarks. The cost to develop a world class trademark can take many years and ultimately require a billion dollars. In fact, Philip Morris spent over $2 billion in 1989 alone just to support and maintain its portfolio of valuable brand names. The cost in the United States simply to introduce a new trademark is approximately $20 million. Corporate raiders are currently buying established trademarks at less cost than the amount required to develop a new one. A trademark that has captured the trust and loyalty of consumers usually commands premium pricing. Application of this valuable characteristic to other products and services can generate new sources of earning power. Corporations that are not pursuing such opportunities find themselves acquisition targets of those that *can* recognize the possibilities.

---

**Key Investment Concept # 3**

Synergy in the 1990s and beyond will focus on the exploitation of intangible assets.

---

Demand for full exploitation of intangible assets is driven by an atmosphere of impatience that pervades the investment community. Despite all the evils attributed to corporate raiders, a primary benefit is a revitalized attitude among management toward corporate value.

It is widely accepted that one of the best defenses against an unwanted takeover is the maintenance and proliferation of a high stock price. Maintaining a high stock price requires that the economic returns from corporate investments be maximized. Intangible assets are receiving the greatest amount of attention toward achieving this goal. Unlike the specific products or services that a company produces, intangible assets often possess potential for exploitation beyond their original utilization. Trademarks and technology are prime examples. Chapter 8 focuses on the methods to maximize stock value which will be prevalent in future corporate planning.

Many acquisitions are now based on the perception that additional opportunities exist for extension of trademarks into related and sometimes unrelated fields. Incremental exploitation of this intangible asset can be achieved separately from its original utilization.

Patented technology and the ability to generate additional technological advantages are additional forms of valuable intangible assets. Corporations that already possess strong trademarks are purchasing organizations that can produce new products on which the well recognized name can be placed.

Even retail sites are an intangible asset that some corporations find highly desirable. Hechinger, a chain of hardware stores, purchased Bradlees, a Northeast chain of discount department stores. The stores were all quickly closed and converted to hardware stores. The attraction for Hechinger's was the intangible asset possessed by Bradlees in the form of desirable retail sites in high income residential areas where room for additional commercial space was limited.

## Legal Attitudes Enhance Value

Enhanced legal protection around the world has made patents and trademarks more valuable than ever before. Chapter 6 provides a detailed discussion about how the legal system has enhanced the value of intangible assets. In the United States the patent system was dramatically strengthened with the creation of the Court of Appeals of the Federal Circuit (CAFC). It is the only court in the nation that handles patent and trademark case appeals. The continuity of the court's thinking and decisions has strengthened the rights of patent and trademark owners. It has made willful infringement a very risky proposition. Damage awards by courts are higher than ever before. Lost profit awards of up to 60% of the infringing sales have been upheld by the CAFC. Damage awards based on a reasonable royalty have used royalty rates as high as 25% of sales. Several decisions have upheld damage awards that have bankrupted the infringer. Patent rights have been reinforced to such an extent that the value of patents has risen to new heights. The exploitation opportunities of licensing are greatly enhanced and royalty income has risen as a result. In just the last four years Texas Instrument has earned over $650 million from patent licensing.

The enhanced protection has trebled the avenues by which intangible assets can safely be exploited. Instead of only deriving profits from internal use, the licensing option is now well protected and joint venture projects are becoming common. Instead of deriving only one stream of income form intangible assets we are more likely to see three: internal use, licensing, and joint ventures. Each of these represents another source of earnings growth, which adds to the value of companies.

Legal protection of intangible assets is not limited to the United States. Germany, Great Britain, Japan, and France are all providing strong legal protection for intangible assets. Even the third world recognizes the importance of protecting these vital assets. IBM was successful recently in stopping five companies within the People's Republic of China from assembling knock-offs of their IBM PC. More than 3800 trademark infringement cases were processed last year in five of China's provinces.

Legal protection around the world is advancing in recognition that intangible assets are the most important asset and must be protected. The value of patents and trademarks as a result are enhanced along with the opportunities to expand economic exploitation and increase corporate value.

## Accounting Statements Miss the Point

Accounting rules around the world differ greatly and in the United States, as discussed in Chapter 9, they are completely inadequate with respect to intangible assets. Balance sheets very often do not even identify the existence of keystone patents or world class trademarks. These assets are the source of premium product pricing and market share dominance, yet the value of these vital corporate assets are altogether absent from financial statements.

Intangible assets capture market share, support product pricing premiums, and present the greatest flexibility for expansion into new ventures. Yet, some accounting practices include these assets while others do not.

Discovering intangible assets isn't always easy. For most investors, annual reports serve as the chief source of information about a company. Unfortunately, the existence and value of the vital intangible assets is rarely included. Financial statements are usually audited by a certified public accountant, providing information about the financial condition of the company as well as the historic trend of performance and profits. Income statements show sales and expenses, leading to a presentation of earnings. Balance sheets present the total assets and liabilities of the company. Neither can be relied on to properly present intangible assets.

The asset side of the balance sheet does not include intangible assets. Assets are separated into current assets and long-term assets. Cash, inventories, accounts receivable, and prepaid expenses are the most typical current assets. Long-term assets include the land, buildings, and machinery used in manufacturing products. Search as hard as you like, but intangible assets are only included when they have been acquired and even then only under certain conditions. The intangible assets that were developed and cultivated over decades are completely omitted.

## Care and Feeding of Intangibles

Fundamental analysis of market share, earnings forecasts, and competitive forces is a fine practice but ignores the underlying health of the intangible assets that are the foundation of value. An important theme presented in Chapter 7 is the fragile nature of intangible assets. Trademarks must always be supported by advertising expenditures and technology must continuously be advanced and renewed. An analysis of advertising expenses and research spending supports this point. Evidence is also presented to show the consequences of neglecting the advertising and research efforts. Once again, significant changes to investment values are the result of proper care and feeding.

What happens to the value of a company when intangible assets are not continually advanced? Most of the time value suffers. It is often tempting for management to boost earnings in an off year by eliminating a substantial portion of the R&D budget or ad spending. Current earnings will indeed benefit from a reduction of these expenses but long-term profitability may suffer for a prolonged period. Once market share is lost it is difficult to regain it from the competitors. In 1985, General Foods eliminated advertising on Maxwell House coffee in order to improve short-term earnings. Market share dropped by an enormous 10 share points (each share point represents 1% of the total market) and has only recently been recaptured by a revitalized and expensive advertising campaign. Following the trends of ad spending is very important because it represents trademark support and maintenance.

The same is true for technology. Obsolescence is always nearby as competitors try to build a better mousetrap. The amounts that are spent on research and development are also reported in 10Ks and should be reviewed to be sure that adequate support is being provided for the continuation of technological advantages. Adequate amounts of R&D for one industry can be abysmal for another. One way to detect if R&D spending is adequate is to compare the amounts that a company has historically spent with the current levels. If the amount is dropping, this may indicate that the company is resting on its laurels and has become more interested in earnings management through expense controls. Another test is to compare the amounts of R&D with successful competitors. If the company being studied compares poorly, then its future prospects may be limited as other companies surpass it technologically.

**The Trend Is Clear**

Popular business periodicals are beginning to focus on the new intangible asset investment trend. A recent article in *INC* magazine explains how a consultant at Coopers & Lybrand, a Big Six accounting firm, focuses on intangible assets when valuing closely held companies. *The Wall Street Journal* recently talked about how the toy company Mattel uses an acquisition strategy that focuses on strong brand names. *Personal Investor* and *Registered Representative*, both investment magazines, featured articles recently that focused on intangible asset investing. Prentice-Hall featured a discussion about intangible asset investing at a conference entitled *Joint Ventures and Other Business Combinations*. The business community is just starting to appreciate the importance of intangible assets. Great profits are available for investors that understand these assets.

## Intangibles Among Traditional CorporateAssets

Chapter 3 introduces the concept of intellectual property and intangible assets as being an integral part of the overall business enterprise. The other assets of a corporation are reviewed (monetary and tangible) along with the idea of how intangible assets are the ultimate corporate "spark plug." Sources of intangible assets are discussed: purchase or create. The main point of Chapter 3 is to stress that intangible assets are not generally recognized as the most important possessions of corporate America. Without intangible assets the corporation is a collection of unintegrated and idle machinery with wandering employees.

A list of key intangible assets is presented along with the relative importance of each type. The list includes some intriguing examples. King World Productions has a balance sheet that looks like a disaster, with negative shareholders' equity, but the company makes extraordinary profits. It possesses intangible assets in the form of distribution rights for *Wheel of Fortune* and other television programs. These assets generate great profits but aren't shown on the balance sheet. The economic benefits that are derived from these assets and others like them are discussed along with the special advantages that are inherent: barriers to competition, premium pricing, and extension to ancillary products.

## The Power of Trademarks

A detailed discussion about trademarks is presented in Chapter 5 and shows where powerful trademarks originate. The costs are dear but the results can be fantastic. The stock performance of a company that owns a portfolio of powerful trademarks is shown as exceeding the general performance of stock indexes. Pre-eminent trademarks are presented and discussed along with a comparison to the big trademarks of 50 years ago. The continuous need to support these assets through advertising is highlighted along with information about the amount of money spent annually on trademark support. The power of trademarks is shown to be customer loyalty and well supported perceptions among customers.

## Strategies Used to Exploit Intangible Assets

Chapter 8 presents the many ways in which companies are able to exploit the intangible assets that they possess, including joint ventures, licensing, and outright sale. The value of a corporation can greatly be enhanced by full and proper exploitation of intangible assets. Merck and Johnson & Johnson are the two largest health care companies in the United States. They have just formed a joint venture to market new over-the-counter medicines. The venture will combine Merck's preeminent research and development operations with Johnson & Johnson's formidable consumer marketing capabilities. This is a classic example of combining two highly valuable types of intangible asset. The technological assets of Merck will be combined with the trademark property of Johnson & Johnson, representing, as described in *The Wall Street Journal*, "an unbeatable combination." Clearly, this potentially valuable venture has little to do with the traditional corporate assets of real estate and machinery.

Companies can make big money with intangible assets even if no fixed assets are owned. Chapter 8 shows that many companies add to their profits by licensing while other companies make all their profits from licensing. Johnson & Johnson just negotiated the biggest deal in history with the British Technology Group to market some of Johnson & Johnson's technology worldwide. Many more companies will follow this lead because enhanced value results.

## Watch Out for High-Tech Story Stocks

The complex nature of certain intangible assets can be very confusing to investors that have stars in their eyes—stars that make them believe that they can be a founding investor in the next Xerox, IBM, or Genentech. Promoters of questionable investments with even more questionable character can push venture capital investments and high-tech initial public offerings that are based on unreasonable expectations. It gets easier for stockbrokers when the high-tech story is complex. Ultimately, the sales pitch boils down to "trust me and I'll make you wealthy." Chapter 11 provides insight to help starry eyed investors stay a little closer to earth. High-tech story stocks can indeed yield enormous profits but the risk must be understood and appreciated. Chapter 10 spells out the risks.

## Ten of the Best

At the end of the book, the final chapter presents some of the best intangible asset company investments.

Throughout this book important concepts are highlighted as Key Investment Concepts. The unique nature of intangible assets may be foreign to many readers. Highlighted information, deemed to be especially important, is presented throughout the book.

## Summary

Corporate value and investment success are dominated more than ever before by transactions that focus on the exploitation of intangible assets. Legal systems around the world are supporting the rights associated with intangible assets. Accounting practices are being tested and adjusted to fully incorporate the importance of these assets in financial statements. Corporate raiders are forcing corporate managers to squeeze more earnings from their keystone patents and world class trademarks. Licensing and joint ventures have only just entered the infancy stage of their potentially long life cycle as the subject of global transactions.

Intangible assets are the foundation of corporate value because they are the ultimate source of earnings, which in turn are the basis of value. *Investors must focus on these hidden assets to find winning stocks and to avoid disaster. Intangible asset investing is the fundamental business trend for the 1990s.*

# 2

# THE FEVER ON
# WALL STREET TO
# ACQUIRE INTANGIBLES

Frenzied merger and acquisition activities have always been part of business with trends and fads evident throughout history. As we enter the 1990s, intangible assets will be the primary focus for the next decade.

Throughout history, government leaders and business giants have coveted the property of others. Merger and acquisition activities have always been propelled by the self-confidence of the buyer or more accurately ego. The belief that acquirers can do a better job of running the show than the current managers is the fundamental force driving acquisitions. Acquirers recognize, or at least think they recognize, opportunities to acquire underperforming businesses and assets from which they will enjoy enhanced profits.

Such opportunities can be brought about by poor management of assets by others, poor company performance where assets are underutilized, and security markets that don't recognize the value that acquirers envision.

Land wars in the Wild West period of U.S. history were replaced by monopoly building which attempted the domination of industries like railroads, oil, and steel. Plant capacity at one time was a coveted property as once were natural resources the delight of bargain hunters. As the nature of the global economy and societal priorities change, the types of coveted property also change. At all times, however, the accumulation of property, often driven by great confidence or bloated ego, has been and will be fundamental to business activities. As this chapter will show, *the coveted crown jewels driving the current fever to acquire are intangible assets.*

## Management Science Magic

In the 1960s acquisitions were driven by diversification and integration strategies. Diversification spread economic risks among many businesses to counter the negative effects of being too focused in cyclical industries. Integration merged manufacturing, raw material suppliers, and distribution networks to bring control and profits from indirectly related activities under one corporate roof.

Manufacturing companies acquired raw material suppliers. Then finance companies and other vaguely related businesses became desirable. As acquisitions hit stride in the 1960s, completely unrelated businesses were combined into a portfolio of diversified business investments. Anything and everything were potential acquisition targets.

The underlying notion was that acquirers would introduce *management* science and centralized control, thereby enhancing the value of all the portfolio components. Management science would be the missing element of magic that would make the combined entities more powerful, successful, and profitable than when the businesses were independent. *Conglomerate* was a descriptive term that managers eagerly sought to have bestowed upon their company. It carried images of power and expansive management skills. With superior organizational skills founded in management science, the acquirers of the 1960s thought that they could manage any business. Understanding the nature of the business didn't matter. Overreaching occurred and conglomerate builders found that more than a little knowledge about the business was needed.

Gulf & Western started life as a manufacturer of automotive parts, but following the fad of the 1960s the company embarked on a buying binge that eventually included completely unrelated business interests:

Paramount Pictures
Desilu Productions
South Puerto Rico Sugar Company
Provident Washington Insurance
Consolidated Cigar Company
Madison Square Garden

ITT managed international telephone systems and manufactured telephone equipment when the portfolio acquisition fever struck in the early 1960s. Before the decade was out, the following dissimilar businesses were part of the ITT conglomerate:

Continental Baking
Avis Car Rental
Sheraton Hotels
Hartford Steam Boiler Insurance
Grinnell

In the 1970s United Airlines sought to build a travel company empire. Acquisitions were made that would integrate all aspects of travel. The collection included:

Hertz Rental Car Company
Hilton Hotels
Westin Hotels

Huge and unwieldy corporate structures were needed just to monitor the performance of the unrelated businesses that comprised these conglomerates. Long delays occurred in decision making and strategy meetings, with *Corporate* killing any inventive ideas developed at the operating level. Often the accounting system used to monitor one of the conglomerate components was completely unworkable for monitoring other components. Management time was spent studying the portfolio rather than managing the business. Instead of gaining investment performance from portfolio diversification, the centralized control structures introduced anti-synergistic costs of time and money. In almost all cases the conglomerates have failed. Stock performance for these portfolios of management science was dismal. Companies soon learned that management science magic was a false deity. Conglomerates were dismantled and managers did everything possible to shed the dark shadow that accompanied the once coveted descriptive word—conglomerate.

## Excess Asset Magic

Acquisitions of the late 1970s and early 1980s focused on the value of excess assets. These assets were on the balance sheet but were not adequately reflected in the stock price. They included real estate, cash hoards, and resource reserves like timberland and oil, especially oil.

Companies that had excess assets were the delight of acquirers who wanted to restructure and enhance. If the excess asset was cash, the company could be acquired and the cash issued as a special dividend or used to pay-down the debt associated with the purchase of the company. If the excess asset was real estate, then after acquiring the company sale-leasebacks were put into effect. Valuable land and buildings were sold to institutional investors as safe investments providing the acquired company with cash. A long-term lease allowed the company to continue to use the property.

In the case of oil, acquirers went on a binge.

T. Boone Pickens, Jr. was trained as a petroleum geologist. In the late 1970s, the cost to find oil was at about $15 per barrel and oil prices were rising as fast as the OPEC nations could schedule price-fixing conferences. The stock exchange became an easier place to search for oil reserves than the Indonesian jungles. The stock market was perceived to be undervaluing the stocks of asset-rich companies. On the stock exchange the cost could be as a low as $5 per barrel if

*Exhibit 2-1*   Major Mergers and Acquisitions of the Early 1980s ($ billions)

| Acquirer | Target | Price | Year |
|----------|--------|-------|------|
| Chevron | Gulf | $13.2 | 1984 |
| Texaco | Getty | $10.1 | 1984 |
| DuPont | Conoco | $8.0 | 1981 |
| U.S. Steel | Marathon Oil | $6.6 | 1982 |
| Mobil Oil | Superior | $5.7 | 1984 |
| U.S. Steel | Husky Oil | $3.6 | 1986 |

the deal were priced right. Exhibit 2-1 lists some of the biggest deals that occurred in the early 1980s. They were almost all founded on the fever to acquire excess assets.

As with all good ideas, other people quickly see the benefits and join the party. Bidding wars erupt, bargains disappear, and the game abruptly ends.

## Financing Magic

The most recent acquisition fever has been fueled by the idea that a little more debt and a willingness to accept just a little more risk would shower profits on those that knew how to introduce financing magic. Acquirers during this period focused on the introduction of financing capabilities, once again not caring about the business they were buying and often not even understanding the business.

Leveraged buy-outs (LBOs) fueled acquisitions during the late 1980s. Raiders looked to enhance investments by using more aggressive financial structures, and at times the restructuring made a lot of sense. LBOs combined an aggressive leverage strategy with the excess asset concept. Instead of gaining access to particular assets like cash and real estate, takeover artists focused on entire business units that they considered as undervalued or completely unrepresented in the stock price of the target company.

Initially, it can be argued that raiders contributed in a positive way to corporate America. Leverage buy-outs provided a means to get corporate America back on track. Overbloated corporate executives that ignored shareholders just had to go. They spent money on lavish perks, gave themselves extraordinary bonuses, even in poor performance years, and acted more like caretakers. It seemed that the attitude of corporate managers was: "Why take risks when mediocrity can get you eight-figure compensation packages?"

LBOs provided a means to get rid of these timid managers and return America's business power to the hands of managers that had a financial stake in the business success. Once again, however, good ideas are often extended far beyond realistic applications. Early successes in LBOs caught the attention of many raiders. Bidding wars erupted again and the bargains disappeared. Watching the devastating effect of "just a little" more debt is going to be a sad legacy of the 1980s.

The focus, however, has finally changed.

## Look at What They Are Buying: The Magic of Intangible Assets

It seems that management leaders have finally returned to a tight business focus. Possibly the LBO debt burdens hanging around many necks have forced clear thinking as to how to get the most out of the businesses they know best. A review of some of the biggest deals that occurred in the late 1980s displays an interesting contrast to the focus of earlier years. Exhibit 2-2 shows that the takeover action has shifted to the acquisition of intangible assets.

*Exhibit 2-2*   Major Mergers and Acquisitions of the Early 1980s ($ billions)

| Acquirer | Target | Price | Year |
|---|---|---|---|
| RJR Nabisco | LBO | $25.0 | 1989 |
| Philip Morris | Kraft | $13.4 | 1988 |
| Campeau | Federated Department Stores | $7.4 | 1988 |
| General Electric | RCA | $6.4 | 1986 |
| Beatrice Foods | LBO | $6.2 | 1986 |
| Philip Morris | General Foods | $5.6 | 1985 |
| Grand Metropolitan | Pillsbury | $5.5 | 1988 |
| Sante Fe | Southern Pacific | $5.1 | 1983 |
| Kodak | Sterling Drugs | $5.1 | 1988 |
| Allied | Signal | $4.9 | 1985 |
| R. J. Reynolds | Nabisco | $4.9 | 1985 |
| Burroughs | Sperry | $4.8 | 1986 |
| General Motors | Hughes Aircraft | $4.7 | 1985 |
| Capital Cities | ABC | $3.5 | 1985 |

When Philip Morris decided to diversify, the company could have purchased anything that it wanted. Their billion dollar war chest of cash from cigarette profits made all things possible. With the entire business world as possibilities, in what assets did Philip Morris decide to invest? Brand names. Like a collection of great art, Philip Morris has assembled an investment in the strongest, best known, most valuable brand names in the world: brand names that have been part of everyone's life including rights of passage. Acquisitions of Kraft and General Foods were the methods used to start the collection. The portfolio includes Marlboro cigarettes, Miller beer, Jello-O gelatin, Post cereal, Kool-Aid, Maxwell House coffee, Oscar Meyer hot dogs, Breyer's and Sealtest ice cream, Velveeta cheese, and Miracle Whip salad dressing.

Grand Metropolitan is a foreign corporation that also had a strong financial position with which to acquire. Their strategy was to enter the United States in a big way. They also decided to build a portfolio of brand names. They acquired Pillsbury.

Kodak set out on a diversification strategy. Patented drugs with FDA approvals were its target when it acquired Sterling Drugs.

R.J. Reynolds was another cigarette company with huge amounts of tobacco profits. With all things being possible, the company, like Philip Morris, also chose to invest in the brand names of Nabisco.

General Motors elected a diversification strategy and decided to acquire the high technology of Hughes Aircraft.

## The Brand Names of RJR Nabisco

Intangible assets were the foundation of the largest acquisition of all time. RJR Nabisco was acquired in 1989 by Kohlberg, Kravis, Roberts and Company (KKR) for $25 billion. The company is a dominant force in the tobacco and food industries with consolidated sales of $17 billion for 1988. The most important and valuable assets that were obtained involve internationally recognized brand names.

In 1913 the company introduced the first national brand name cigarette, Camel. With the addition over decades of Winston, Salem, Doral, and Vantage, RJR controls almost 30% of the cigarette market. Food business brand names owned by RJR include Oreo, Ritz,

Chips Ahoy, Premium, Fleischmann's Blue Bonnet, Grey Poupon, Milk Bone, Ortega, Shredded Wheat, Peek Freans, Hawaiian Punch, Del Monte, Planters, Life Savers, Baby Ruth, *and* Butter Fingers.

Substantially all the domestic cigarette production of RJR along with 25% of the foreign sales volume is manufactured at facilities in the Winston-Salem, North Carolina area. Manufacturing locations are also maintained in Belgium, Brazil, Canada, Canary Islands, Ecuador, Hong Kong, Malaysia, Puerto Rico, Switzerland, and West Germany. The distribution of cigarettes is accomplished directly to chain stores and retail outlets, and indirectly to other retail locations through a network of distributors. The company has direct contact with over 300,000 retail accounts.

The food business was acquired instead of created, like the cigarette business. Major acquisitions included Del Monte in 1979 and Nabisco Brands in 1985. Nabisco is one of the largest packaged food companies in the world. Products include cookies, crackers, snack foods, hot cereals, margarine, pet foods, dry-mix desserts, and other grocery products. Del Monte is the leading producer in the United States of fruits and vegetables.

The vast array of physical assets that are part of the RJR Nabisco empire include almost every conceivable asset that a corporation could hope to own. In just one facility at Tobaccoville, North Carolina the plant covers 2 million square feet filled with the most technologically advanced cigarette manufacturing equipment in the world. In contrast, the average manufacturing facility is well under 100,000 square feet. Just think of all the desks, copy machines, delivery trucks, conveyor belts, cigarette machines, warehouse racks, office buildings, company cars, private aircraft, tools, tobacco inventory, storage freezers, farm equipment, packaging machines, food mixers, lift trucks, and endless miscellaneous items located around the world. Surprisingly, these physical properties make up a minor portion of the total assets purchased. *All the buildings and equipment around the world accounted for less than 20% of the $25 billion price tag.*

To fully appreciate the transformation of the balance sheet AFTER the deal, a little bit of accounting background is needed here. Later, in Chapter 9, flaws and weaknesses in the accounting system with regard to intangible assets are discussed in detail.

## Accounting for the RJR Nabisco Purchase Price

When RJR Nabisco was acquired, the buyer got all the company assets in exchange for the purchase price of $25 million. Exhibit 2-3 shows a comparison of balance sheets for RJR Nabisco. The first column shows the balance sheet amounts for the year-end December 31, 1988. This balance sheet represents the last full year for the company BEFORE the KKR leveraged buy-out. The amounts shown under the December 31, 1989 column represent the balance sheet for RJR Nabisco Holdings Corporation, a corporation that was created to effect the acquisition of RJR Nabisco, Inc. along with limited partnerships of KKR and other holding companies. The 1989 column represents the accounting of the assets for the company AFTER the buy-out. A comparison of the two balance sheets shows the importance ascribed to the intangible assets.

AFTER the acquisition a balance sheet was established to show the assets owned and the liabilities owed. To satisfy a most important accounting rule, the value of the assets must balance the liabilities and equity. The balance sheet must show the value of the assets that were obtained with the invested funds. They must be equal to the invested funds. Regardless of the original value basis of assets on the BEFORE balance sheet, when the AFTER balance sheet is compiled the asset values can be *stepped-up* to their market value. Step-up is a term that accounts for the larger values that are typically associated with revalued assets after an acquisition. Revalued assets are placed on the AFTER balance sheet at market value. This is usually higher than the BEFORE amount, which has been distorted by accounting procedures. Analysis of the RJR Nabisco balance sheet AFTER the acquisition shows that almost $24 billion of the total assets acquired were trademarks and other intangible assets.

The BEFORE and AFTER balance sheets show the assets and liabilities of RJR but the substantial intangible assets are not fully identified until AFTER.

*Cash and Short-term Investments* are very liquid assets that the company can use almost immediately. Unexpected expenses can be satisfied with this asset and temporary shortfalls in operating cash flow can be covered. While policies differ among companies, most do not keep excessive amounts of cash on hand. Profits are either paid to

*Exhibit 2-3*   RJR Nabisco, Inc. Balance Sheet Comparison Before and After the Buy-Out ($ millions)

| Assets: | BEFORE 12/31/88 | Percent | AFTER 12/31/89 | Percent |
|---|---|---|---|---|
| Cash & Short–term Investments | 1,425 | 8% | 142 | 0% |
| Accounts & Notes Receivable | 1,920 | 11% | 998 | 3% |
| Inventories | 2,571 | 14% | 2,876 | 8% |
| Prepaid Expenses and Excise Taxes | 265 | 1% | 358 | 1% |
| Net Assets Available For Sale | 0 | 0% | 2,300 | 6% |
| Total Current Assets | 6,181 | 35% | 6,674 | 18% |
| Property, Plant & Equipment – at cost | 8,363 | 47% | 5,436 | 15% |
| Less Accumulated Depreciation | 2,214 | 12% | 417 | 1% |
| Net Property, Plant & Equipment | 6,149 | 35% | 5,019 | 14% |
| Trademarks and Other Intangible Assets | 4,555 | 26% | 23,736 | 65% |
| Other Assets & Deferred Charges | 866 | 5% | 983 | 3% |
| Total Assets | 17,751 | 100% | 36,412 | 100% |
| Liabilities: | | | | |
| Notes Payable | 423 | 2% | 181 | 0% |
| Accounts Payable & Accrued Expenses | 3,220 | 18% | 3,265 | 9% |
| Current Maturities of Long Term Debt | 337 | 2% | 2,632 | 7% |
| Income Taxes Accrued | 300 | 2% | 490 | 1% |
| Total Current Liabilities | 4,280 | 24% | 6,568 | 18% |
| Long Term Debt | 4,975 | 28% | 21,948 | 60% |
| Other Noncurrent Liabilities | 1,617 | 9% | 2,873 | 8% |
| Deferred Income Taxes | 1,060 | 6% | 3,786 | 10% |
| Redeemable Preferred Stock | 125 | 1% | 0 | 0% |
| Common Shareholders' Equity | 5,694 | 32% | 1,237 | 3% |
| Total Liabilities & Equity | 17,751 | 100% | 36,412 | 100% |

### Business Enterprise Components:

| | BEFORE 12/31/88 | Percent | AFTER 12/31/89 | Percent |
|---|---|---|---|---|
| Net Working Capital | 1,901 | 14% | 106 | 0% |
| Fixed Assets | 6,149 | 46% | 5,019 | 17% |
| Intangible Assets | 5,421 | 40% | 24,719 | 83% |
| Total B E V | 13,471 | 100% | 29,844 | 100% |

shareholders as dividends or reinvested in research or plant expansions. Cash assets are similar to the money that individuals keep as a checkbook balance just in case something happens. Serious money is usually spent or invested. As of December 31, 1988 RJR had $1.4 billion of cash and short-term assets. The new owners used more than $1.3 million of the rainy day reserves to help finance the acquisition, leaving only $142 million on the AFTER balance sheet.

*Accounts and Notes Receivable* show the amounts that are owed to the company and that are expected to be received within the year. Typically, payment is received in 60 days. Customers promise to pay at a later date for products that have been delivered. The aggregate of these promises is the accounts receivable asset. BEFORE the acquisition RJR showed $1.9 billion. AFTER accounts receivable dropped to just under $1 billion. Two reasons are most likely for this $1 billion decrease. First, the new owners had great incentive, in the form of a huge debt burden, to take steps to speed along the collection process. Discount offers could have encouraged customers to make quicker payments, thereby reducing the accounts receivable balance. Second, more than a few subsidiaries and business units of the acquired company were divested along with the associated accounts receivable. European food units were sold in June 1989 for $2.5 billion. Chun King was also sold in June for $52 million. A Scandinavian food unit was sold in July 1989 for $20.4 million. Del Monte Tropical Fruit was sold in September 1989 for $875 million. Del Monte Foods canned food units were put on the block as well in September 1989. Proceeds from the sale also have helped to feed the leverage buy-out debt monster. When these businesses were sold, accounts receivable that were associated with the respective businesses went along with the business and were removed from the RJR balance sheet.

*Inventories* are raw materials waiting to be converted into products or finished product waiting to be sold to customers. Raw materials for RJR include tobacco leaf, cigarette packaging materials, wheat, sugar, chocolate, peanuts, fruit, and thousands of other items that are used in the cigarette and food business. BEFORE and AFTER the deal the company had over $2.5 billion invested in inventories.

*Prepaid Expenses and Taxes* are usually a minor item. Represented here are the amounts paid for services and taxes in advance of the bill. Not much changed in this minor category.

*Net Assets Available for Sale* is a new current asset category presenting the value of business units and subsidiaries that are planned for divestiture within the next 12 months. Obviously, the new owners have identified $2.3 billion worth of assets and business units that are now considered unnecessary or undesirable for helping to meet the new strategic plan, which must clearly center on surviving debt obligations. On the BEFORE balance sheet these assets were categorized with long-term assets as part of the categories stated below current assets. AFTER the deal they were reclassified as current assets because the proceeds are expected to be received within 1 year.

Overall, the total value of current assets was little changed BEFORE and AFTER the deal.

*Property, Plant, and Equipment* shown at the original cost (the amount that was paid for the assets when originally purchased, constructed, or acquired) does not seem to have changed significantly at first glance. Building, production machinery, delivery trucks, and all other fixed assets are included in this category. RJR showed almost $8.4 billion as the original cost for the physical property BEFORE the buy-out. After allowing for accumulated depreciation, the net accounting value for fixed assets is $6.1 billion. Accumulated depreciation is the aggregate of the annual depreciation expenses taken over the life of the assets, which account for the continuing deterioration of the property resulting from usage and wear and tear. The net amount supposedly represents the depreciated value of the used property.

AFTER the acquisition this amount dropped to $5 billion. Part of the reason for the decrease is the removal of assets that were divested as part of business units. Other fixed assets were reclassified as part of the $2.3 billion of Net Assets Available for Sale. Also, the amount of accumulated depreciation since the new balance sheet was established is a substantially lower $417 million. Overall, the fixed asset values of RJR did not change dramtically.

*Other Assets and Deferred Charges* were minor amounts both BEFORE and AFTER the deal. They represent a hodgepodge of assets that do not fit into other asset categories.

The serious money on the AFTER balance sheet is attributed to the intangible assets of RJR. Trademarks and other intangible assets were shown at $4.6 billion BEFORE the acquisition and almost **$24**

**billion** AFTER the deal. This represents 65% of total assets and an astounding 83% of the invested capital.

One year after the acquisition, the amount of invested capital (long-term debt and shareholders' equity) totaled almost $30 billion as shown at the bottom of Exhibit 2-3. Net working capital (current assets less current liabilities), fixed assets, and intangible assets are the property that was received. Trademarks and other intangibles dominate the business. These intangible assets didn't just appear as alchemy of the leveraged buy-out. They were part of the company all along, but since intangible assets that have been created in-house are not recorded on the balance sheet, some of the most valuable trademarks in the world were never recorded as assets. RJR Nabisco was an acquisition of intangible assets. It can even be argued that the acquisition could not have been completed successfully without the existence of these worldwide trademarks.

### Other Intangible Assets That I Want Now

Joseph J. McAlinden, research director at Dillon Read & Co., told *Business Week*, December 25, 1989, "What we'll see in 1990 are more rational takeovers; acquisitions where a company in one industry wants to buy another's brand name, sales force or market dominance."

Opportunities to make profits by investing in takeover stocks will still exist. Poor management, poor company performance, or sleepy security markets that undervalue a stock will still exist. A new focus for the 1990s, however, will be introduced. Intangible assets will rule the decade.

Television home shopping became big business in the early 1980s with the creation of the Home Shopping Network. The industry has seen sales grow from about $1 million in 1980 to $1 billion in 1988. QVC Network acquired CVN Companies in 1989 for $432 million. The companies have a combined viewership of 37 million households. Intangible assets desired: access to customers.

Spiegel is the largest direct mail-order house in the country and has five million active customers. Spiegel added to its customer base with the acquisition of Eddie Bauer, a marketer of outdoor wear, and Honeybee, a seller of women's clothing. In both cases, the attraction was the brand name recognition and the list of additional active customers.

In October 1989, Ploygram, Inc., a record company, paid $500 million for A&M Records which includes Janet Jackson and Sting as part of the stable of artists under contract. The acquisition did not include any manufacturing capabilities or any distribution network: just the intangible assets of artist contracts and a collection of hot record albums.

Ford can obviously build any type of car that it wants. But it can't necessarily penetrate new markets without brands. So Jaguar PLC was purchased to give the company an entry into the upscale luxury car market. Intangible assets desired: the Jaguar brand name.

Coors Brewing Company paid $425 million for Stroh Brewing Company. The list of brands include Stroh's, Stroh's Light, Signature, Schlitz (which was at one time the best selling beer in the United States), Schlitz Light, Schlitz Malt Liquor, Schaefer, Schaefer Light, Old Milwaukee, Goebel, Red Bull, Silver Thunder, and St. Bart's. Licensing rights for Piel's also were among the intangible assets acquired.

Campeau Corporation owns Allied Stores Corp. and Federated Department Stores. Operating units comprise almost 500 stores, including Jordan Marsh, Mass Brothers, Stern's, The Bon, Bloomingdale's, Abraham & Straus, Burdine's, Lazarus, Ralph's, and Rich's. In September 1989, Robert Campeau filed for bankruptcy. Sometimes the intangible asset takeover fever gets way out of hand.

It almost seems that any independent company with a portfolio of consumer brand names is a takeover target—profitable or not.

Bertelsmann AG bought the money losing RCA and Arista records group in 1985 for $300 million. It got Mili Vanilli and Whitney Houston. Intangible asset desired: artist contracts.

## Buying Other People's Technology

Spending on research and development has lagged far behind the amounts spent to acquire, as shown in Exhibit 2-4.

Throughout the 1970s industry spending for research and development was about equal to the amounts that were spent on

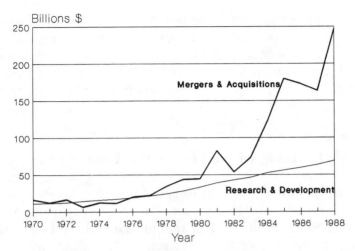

*Exhibit 2-4*    More Spending on Mergers than R&D

mergers and acquisitions. In the late 1970s, however, the spending lines on the graph departed, never to cross paths again. To replace the innovative intangible assets that were not researched, companies are now in the acquisition marketplace trying to buy the technological assets of others.

The $100 billion pharmaceutical industry is an excellent example of this trend. Bristol-Myers has merged with Squibb; Merrel Dow purchased Marion Laboratories; SmithKline acquired Beecham; and more combinations are likely. One of the primary reasons involves the runaway research costs and 10 year time period needed to discover a new drug, conduct testing, gain regulatory approvals, and mount new marketing efforts. The price tag for such efforts is estimated to be about $200 million per new drug. By the time regulatory approval is achieved, the remaining amount of the 17 year patent protection is only 7 years. Add in the risk that successful drug discoveries are not guaranteed for each research effort and it's easy to see why acquiring established technology is faster and less risky.

Reduced R&D spending is of course a short-term and narrow view. A shortage of future technology is likely, which in turn creates additional investment opportunities. Companies that continue to invest in new technologies and that hone their ability to continually generate new discoveries will be the coveted intangible asset acquisition players of the future. The future of acquisitions will focus on companies that can help fill the void that has been created while management has been playing dangerously with balance sheets. Technologies that exist will of course be popular targets but also companies that can keep the technology pipeline filled are going to be in great demand.

## Strategic Planning with an Intangible Basis

The future of acquisitions is going back to strategy. Financial machinations are not going to be common. The results may not be a whole lot better but at least buyers will have to have a plan for exploitation of intangible assets. Corporate managers have changed their strategic plans away from diversification and portfolio management to a tight focus on the businesses that they know best.

A brief review of almost any annual report includes a message from The Chairman of the Board about the strategic plans for the future. More than ever these plans include intangible asset acquisitions.

In the Colgate-Palmolive 1989 annual report, the message is clear. "Colgate's strategy for growth in the 1990s is to concentrate its resources on core [products] categories and to expand consumer brand equities throughout the world...Our growth strategy also involves the acquisition of brands, products, and technology."

Sir Deny Henderson, chairman of ICI, stated: "Our strategies can be simply stated: to be thoroughly competitive in everything we do . . . having distinctive commercial and technological strengths." His plans include acquisitions of commercial strengths and technology: "where we can acquire sound companies which fit our strategy we will do so."

Emerson Electric Company stated in their 1989 annual report that "over the last 10 years, acquisitions, divestitures, and product/market reposturing have given the company a balanced product offering in key business areas...Looking to the future, the company will rely on new products and technology, utilizing the strong technological base to develop new products that are vital to growth."

**Investor Focus**

Takeover stocks can be an interesting investment play, especially if the company has good underlying fundamentals. The desirable take-over stocks of the future are going to be those that possess intangible assets and those that have the ability to create more of them. Investors that want to buy before the company goes into play should begin to focus on intangible assets like brand names and technology.

Colgate is going to acquire brands, ICI wants to capture technology, and Emerson has been acquiring new products and technology all along. The trend is clear. Intangible assets will dominate the focus of business in the 1990s and beyond. The place for individuals to find rewarding investment opportunities requires the same focus. The rest of this book helps to show the way.

---

Key Investment Concept # 4

Takeover stocks in the future will be the ones that have an asset portfolio dominated by intangible assets.

---

# 3

# INTANGIBLES HIDDEN AMONG TRADITIONAL CORPORATE ASSETS

Investment focus is changing. Management science magic, excess asset magic, and financing black magic are finished. Investment success in the coming decade and beyond will be fueled by exploitation of the assets presented in this chapter—intangible asset magic.

Interest is returning to companies with strong fundamentals and earnings growth. James Awad, president of BMI Capital, a money management firm, said in a recent *Wall Street Journal* interview that "more investors are thinking of companies in terms of earnings potential, rather than buy-out value and more investors are taking a closer look at younger, smaller companies whose earnings are growing at rapid rates." He states that investment "safety may not mean owning stocks of big companies with predictable earnings, but rather stocks of companies, both large and small, which have strong *franchises* and *innovative products* that assure earnings strength in a sluggish economy." In broad terms, Awad is referring to intangible assets.

This chapter provides the missing details about intangible assets that are too often broadly defined by vague and imprecise terms. Examples are discussed and the importance of intangible assets to investment success is highlighted. Specifically defined is the vague term of *franchise*. This term implies a favorable characteristic but is all too often bandied about in the investment community with little consideration for its true meaning. Also, the term *goodwill* is going to be exposed as an empty property that is really comprised of many intangible assets.

First, the business framework within which intangible assets are used is presented.

## Business Enterprise Overview

Powerful economic contributions by intangible assets are not possible for the most part outside the business enterprise framework. Various complementary assets must be brought to bear. The system in which intangible assets contribute extraordinary earnings power is commonly referred to as the *business enterprise.* Exhibit 3-1 presents the fundamental components.

Comprised of working capital, tangible assets, and intangible assets, all property of a company falls into one of these three categories.

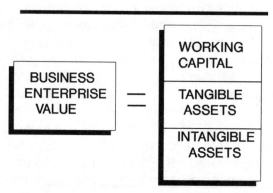

*Exhibit 3-1*    Composition of the Business Enterprise

Net working capital is the net amount of current assets offset by current liabilities. Typical current assets include cash, accounts receivable, inventories, and prepaid expenses. Current liabilities are amounts that the company must pay within the next 12 months, such as accounts payable, accrued expenses, deferred compensation, and the current portion of long-term debt. Chapter 9 provides a detailed discussion of all balance sheet components. For now, think of net working capital as the net amount that must be invested to acquire inventories and begin selling products and services.

Tangible assets, also called fixed assets, are the property of the business that can be touched. Included are buildings, production machinery, computers, trucks, office equipment, and the other tools used to make, sell, and deliver products. These are the assets that store inventory, convert raw materials, process invoices, and control operations.

After cash is invested and the machines are installed, the facility is filled with bright light and hope as the electricians turn on the power. Light bounces off the proud industrial manufacturing monsters and employees rush from the parking lot into the building. The facility is posed for greatness, ready to churn-out . . . what?

Until intangible assets are present nothing else can happen. Missing are the production procedures, assembly drawings, product designs, consumer demand, sales procedures, and distribution methods. Some of the missing intangible assets are mundane operating procedures that control the flow of materials and keep track of operations. Others are powerful forces that command market share, generate premium pricing, and stand as barriers to competitors. In fact, without these powerful intangibles many tangible asset investments are doomed to yield poor investment returns, as will be shown in Chapter 4.

Intangible assets are the spark plugs that bring the sleepy tangible asset investment engine to thunderous and profitable life.

## Essential Characteristics

Most valuable intangible assets provide an *economic advantage* in the form of lower manufacturing or operating costs, such as the following:

1.  Enabling the use of low cost materials.
2.  Enabling the use of less material.
3.  Reducing the amount of labor required to manufacture, inspect, package, or account for a product.
4.  Reducing shipping costs by creating a product that is lighter, smaller, or specially shaped.
5.  Producing higher manufacturing speeds.
6.  Reducing waste or rejects.
7.  Reducing the fuel or electric power requirements.
8.  Eliminating or reducing environmental hazards or improving safety conditions.
9.  Commanding premium pricing.
10. Controlling dominant market share positions.

*Barriers* to competition are also an important aspect of intangible assets. Intangible assets confront competitors with formidable obstacles. Development time may be a barrier. Huge research costs may be a barrier. The absence of important background skills may be a barrier. Whatever the reason, intangible assets contribute great value when they represent a barrier to competition. Such barriers can allow intangible asset owners to control market share and set sustainable premium prices.

## Spark Plug Assets

The rest of this chapter describes some of the most important examples of intangible assets. An appreciation of these assets is important for investors that wish to conduct true fundamental analysis. Understanding the strategy of a company along with its strengths and

---

Key Investment Concept #5

Thorough fundamental analysis of a company requires full understanding of the character and nature of the intangible assets that the company owns.

---

weaknesses requires that the nature of its intangible assets be well understood.

Exhibit 3-2 lists some of the most important intangible assets that a company can possess.

## Intellectual Property

The term *intellectual property* is one in general use which usually refers to *patents, trademarks, copyrights,* and *trade secrets, proprietary technology,* or *know-how:* that is, property derived from the mind. This classification of assets is a special category that is protected by our legal system.

A business enterprise that owns intellectual property can either use it directly or transfer interests in the property to others. In a later chapter an examination is presented of the profitable means by which intellectual property can be exploited outside the controlling company. The legal protection afforded intellectual property makes joint ventures and third-party licensing a profitable alternative for intellectual property exploitation. Some companies, like Texas Instruments, enjoy annual incomes of over $100 million from licensing fees.

## Proprietary Technology and Trade Secrets

Two definitions of these properties include the following:

> Any formula, pattern, patentable device or compilation of information which is used in one's business and which gives an opportunity to obtain an advantage over competitors who do not know or use it. It

---

*Exhibit 3-2*    Intangible Asset List

Intellectual property

Patents

Formulas

Technological know-how

Trademarks

Copyrights

Contracts

Customer relationships

Distribution networks

---

may be a formula for a chemical compound, a process of manufacturing, treating or preserving materials, a pattern for a machine or other device, or a list of customers . . . or it may . . . relate to the sale of goods or to other operations in the business such as a code for determining discounts, rebates or other concessions in a price list or catalog, of bookkeeping or other office management. (*Restatement of Torts*)

Any information not generally known in the trade. It may be an unpatented invention, a formula, pattern, machine, process, customer list, . . . or even news (*E. I. DuPont de Nemours & Co.* v. *United States*, 288 F.2d 904 [Ct. Cl. 1969])

Sometimes trade secrets and proprietary technology inventions are not patented in order to avoid making them public. These are potentially the most valuable because trade secrets can be used exclusively by the developer forever. They can also be the most risky. If inadvertently divulged or independently developed by a competitor, the exclusive use of the secret is lost. Competitors can then enter the market with an equivalent product and start a price war that is sure to erode profits.

The formula for Coca-Cola is one of the best examples of a trade secret. Only one or two executives in the company are purported to know the entire formula. It is kept under lock and key. Industrial examples include the manufacture of special alloys for defense weapons and space vehicles or chemical compounds like plastic resins. Trade secrets can also include the proper environment and process for aging wine.

## Patents

There are a number of reasons why the developer of proprietary technology may wish to obtain specific protection by obtaining a patent. The most compelling reason is when large investments have been spent on research and development, the technology appears to have a strong market, and where there are competitors that are likely to pursue similar research.

An important trade-off must be addressed in the patent decision. Keeping the discovery as a trade secret allows perpetual enjoyment of the economic advantages for as long as the secret lasts. At any moment, however, competitors can introduce the exact same technology to your customers if they discover the secret. Competitive pricing will quickly erase the economic advantage. A specialty business that was based on years of research and multi-million dollar experiments can quickly become a commodity business.

Seeking a patent requires disclosure of the invention. In return, the inventor is granted exclusive use of the invention for 17 years. However, after the exclusive period the invention falls into the public domain for use by anyone. Economic advantages are guaranteed only for the exclusive period. This allows time to recover and profit from the initial research expenditures. Without the exclusive period of exploitation it is unlikely that companies would invest in huge R&D programs only to have the new inventions immediately used by competitors.

This is the typical situation in the pharmaceutical industry. In his book, *Patent and Trademark Tactics and Practice*, David A. Burge cites the case of Sir Alexander Fleming who discovered penicillin in 1929:

> He decided against pursuing patent protection so that his discovery could be commercialized without hindrance, and be put into world-wide use as quickly as possible. The result of this fatal folly was that, without the shield of patent protection, no commercial manufacturers could be found who would make the investment needed to find a way to purify the drug and develop techniques needed for manufacture.[1]

It was 14 years later, during World War II, that penicillin was available in commercial quantities. With the current cost of new drug development amounting to as much as $250 million, the exclusive exploitation period provided by the patent system is essential.

## Patent Definition

A patent is the legal process whereby technology is turned into controllable property with defined rights associated with its ownership. A patent is a property right that is granted by the U.S. govern-

---

[1] David A. Burge, *Patent and Trademark Tactics and Practice*, Wiley, New York, 1984, p. 27.

ment to the inventor by action of the Patent and Trademark Office. The right conferred by the patent grant is the right to exclude others from making, using, or selling the invention.

Burge describes a patent as a "negative right." He explains as follows: "While the right of ownership in most personal property is a *positive* right, the right of ownership in a patent is a *negative* right. It is the negative right to exclude others from making, using, or selling the patented invention."[2]

## The Patent Process

The process of obtaining a patent can be very complex and time-consuming. Obtaining a patent involves the following general activities:

1. An application is made to the Commissioner of Patents and Trademarks and includes a description of the patent and the claims sought, a drawing (when appropriate), and a filing fee.

2. When the application is accepted as being complete, it is assigned to an examiner who is knowledgeable about the specific technology. Applications are normally processed in turn.

3. The examiner analyzes the application for compliance with legal requirements and makes a search through prior U.S. and foreign patents on file, as well as in technical literature to see if the invention is new. The examiner reaches a decision as to the patentability of the claimed invention.

4. The applicant is notified in writing of this decision in an Office Action. It is not uncommon for some or all of the claims to be rejected initially.

5. The applicant must request a reconsideration in writing and clearly and completely explain the basis for his or her belief that the examiner has erred in the examination.

6. The application is then reconsidered and a second Office Action is issued.

7. If the patent is not granted, the process may go through a third round, after which the action is usually considered final.

---

[2] See footnote 1.

The process is not easy. It take years to be successful and costs millions. The applicant may appeal an examiner's final rejection to the Board of Patent Appeals and Interferences and, following that, to the Court of Appeals for the Federal Circuit or file a civil action against the Commissioner. The application process can be very lengthy and can involve a long series of written negotiations with the examiner, modifying, adding, or omitting claims. The inventor, faced with continued rejection, can file a new continuation application in order to obtain a longer period in which to modify the original patent application. If a patent is granted under such a continuation, the original filing date is still controlling. It is conceivable that a protracted application process could finally yield a valid patent with an expiration date only months or even days away.

## Patent Categories

*Utility Patent*    Section 101 of the Code provides that "whoever invents or discovers any new and useful process, machine, manufacture, or composition of matter, or any new and useful improvement thereof, may obtain a patent therefore."[3] The word "process" typically refers to industrial or technical processes. "Manufacture" refers to articles that are manufactured, and "composition of matter" relates to mixtures of ingredients or to new chemical compositions. The patented process invented by Procter & Gamble for making chewy cookies that have crunching crusts is an example.

A utility patent has a term of 17 years from the date of issuance.

*Plant Patent*    Patents are also issued for plants. "Whoever invents or discovers and asexually reproduces any distinct and new variety of plant, including cultivated sports, mutants, hybrids, and newly found seedlings, other than a tuber propagated plant or a plant found in an uncultivated state, may obtain a patent therefore."[4] Plant patents also have a term of protection of 17 years. Some of the tomato plants in neighborhood gardens are protected by patents, as are certain types of seed that farmers plant.

*Design Patent*    Design patents are issued for a term of 14 years and are described as follows: "Whoever invents any new, original

---

[3] 35 USC Section 101.
[4] 35 USC Section 161.

and ornamental design for an article of manufacture may obtain a patent therefore."[5] Design patents protect only the appearance of an object, not its utilitarian features. The case of the Macintosh computer is covered by a design patent. No one else can make a computer look the same way without infringing on the Apple Computer patent.

*Animal Patent*    The United States Supreme Court, in a 1980 decision, found that living matter which owes its unique existence to human intervention is patentable subject matter (*Diamond* v. *Chakrabarty*, 447 U.S. 303, 206 USPQ 195). This decision gave guidance to the Patent and Trademark Office Board of Patent Appeals in Ex parte Allen, 2 USPQ2d 1425 in a similar finding. These decisions raised considerable controversy, but the patent process goes on:

> The U.S. Patent Office granted a patent for a genetically engineered mouse, ushering in an era in which private concerns can profit from and control such artificially developed animals . . . Patent Commissioner Donald Quigg said the agency now is considering granting 21 other patents on genetically altered animals . . . However, two bills have been introduced in Congress to place a moratorium on the granting of animal patents.[6]

A patent is personal property and may be sold, mortgaged, licensed, or bequeathed in a will. Since patents must be applied for by individuals, many are assigned to a business enterprise. Such an assignment is recorded in the Patent and Trademark Office. Most corporations whose employees are involved in research that might lead to patentable inventions require that those employees sign an agreement to assign such inventions to the corporation as a condition of employment.

*Pending Patents*    When a patent application has been received by the Patent and Trademark Office, the applicant may identify products containing the invention with the words "Patent Pending" or "Patent Applied For." This action does not provide any protection against infringement, either intentional or unintentional, because

---

[5] 35 USC Section 171.
[6] *The Wall Street Journal*, "Patent for Genetically Altered Mouse Opens Era for Research, Spurs Protest," April 13, 1988.

until the patent is issued its validity is not known. It may, however, discourage copying since, if and when a patent is issued, protection will ensue *from the date of application.*

---

Key Investment Concept #6

Investors should realize that the existence of a patent does not automatically bestow vast wealth on the corporation and shareholders. The invention, process, discovery, or idea that is patented must possess characteristics that fuel economic advantages—either in the form of cost savings or premium pricing.

---

A patent is basically a trade secret that has been disclosed in return for an exclusive period of use.

Individual investors are not usually aware of the detailed information needed to evaluate the trade secret or patent trade-off decision. Company management must make the decision. Investors must beware, however, that when this happens the 17 year clock starts to run.

Very often investment advisors pitch companies that own keystone patents as if the enhanced profits will grow and last forever. It is important to consider the future. What will happen when the patent expires and competitors rush into the market? Trade secrets may not last forever but patents are guaranteed to expire.

## Trademarks

When the Bell System was dismantled, regional operating companies were placed on their own. It is interesting to note that four of the seven moved to disassociate themselves with the well-known "Bell" telephone trademark:

Pacific Telesis
Ameritech
NYNEX
USWest

The remaining companies retained some "Bell" identification:

BellSouth
Bell Atlantic
Southwestern Bell

The tremendous value in the Bell trademark was recognized by some:

The Bell name itself has been a powerful point of contention since the breakup. After the seven regional companies were created, American Telephone & Telegraph Co. fought vigorously and unsuccessfully for the right to use the Bell name as its own.[7]

Others thought differently:

USWest Inc., determined to build a reputation as a trailblazer, plans to drop the Bell name from its three telephone operating companies and take other steps to consolidate their activities with a fresh identity . . . The company said it decided to scrap the 100-year old Bell label because consumers no longer associate the name with technology leadership . . . The bold plan carries big risks. The name change could backfire, adding to confusion in the marketplace.[8]

A television game show found that contestants could not correctly name the so-called "Baby Bells." An article in *The Wall Street Journal* explained:

USWest sometimes is mistaken for an airline, Pacific Telesis for a tropical disease and NYNEX either for a headache remedy or a stock exchange . . . "Becoming a household name is very tough," concedes Jack L. Sommars, executive director of advertising for Denver-based USWest Inc. "It takes a tremendous amount of dollars." . . . Telecommunications consultants estimate that since the breakup of the Bell System in 1984, the Bell operating companies have spent more than $1 billion trying to get their names and messages across.[9]

---

[7] Julie Amparano, "USWest to Combine into One Concern, Drop Bell Name," *The Wall Street Journal,* May 2, 1988, p. 30.

[8] See footnote 7.

[9] *The Wall Street Journal,* "Identity Problems Plague the Baby Bells," May 10, 1988, p. 41.

## Trademark Function

The function of a trademark is to authenticate the origin of goods or services so that the buyer can select those seen in advertisements or previously purchased. Thus trademarks can be thought of as a "guarantee" of a certain level of quality or performance. The most important economic advantage contributed by a trademark comes from the buyer's trust in the name. Customers are often willing to pay a substantial premium price for the characteristics of the product or the service that the name represents. A well recognized trademark is then an asset that can be of considerable value to an enterprise.

Consumers pay a premium price for the assurance that a familiar trademark represents. Why pay the same price for an unbranded tool? The quality may actually be the same but the perception is that a trademark is worth the extra money. Extra profits are the result. In Chapter 5, the enhancement of corporate profits and investor returns is demonstrated. For now, the importance of trademarks can be thought of in terms of comparison. It is a lot easier to get $10,000 for a Rolex watch than for an equivalent quality watch marketed under the Junko name. Likewise, a BMW commands a $40,000 price tag; but how many cars could fetch the same price with the name IOU. As long as the entire premium price isn't spent to advertise and promote the name, which rarely happens, the net amount of premium price goes to the bottom line.

## Trademark Definition

A trademark, as defined in the Trademark Act of 1946, "includes any word, name, symbol, or device or any combination thereof adopted and used by a manufacturer or merchant to identify his goods and distinguish them from those manufactured by others." Exclusive rights to trademarks are obtained by continued use and, when that use includes trade regulated by the federal government, the trademark may be registered by the Patent and Trademark Office.

Registration remains in force for a fixed period, which can be renewed indefinitely as long as the trademark is used in commerce. Unlike a patented invention, a valuable trademark can be used forever.

## The Trademark Process

Trademark applications are filed with the Patent and Trademark Office if federal registration is sought. The application states the date of first use of the trademark, provides specimens of the mark as it appears in commerce, and a drawing of the mark. The date of first use is important because, under current law, that is the date when protection may begin, if the other requirements are met.

A trademark is registered as being applicable to specific products or services and this specification is part of the application for registration. The application is inspected to be sure it conforms to overall specifications, and then a search is made to compare the applicant mark with those already registered. An examination process similar to that of patents ensues. When the mark is accepted, it is published in the trademarks section of the *Official Gazette*. Opposition to the mark may result, and this is addressed by the Trademark and Appeal Board.

As with patents, the Patent and Trademark Office cannot confer any value to a registered trademark. It only records ownership and bestows exclusive rights. The unique value of a trademark comes from the development, sometimes over decades, of consumer perception about product performance, service quality, social status, and other ephemeral characteristics.

## Changing a Good Thing

During 1986 and 1987, a number of public corporations went to considerable expense to change their trademarks. Among these were Primerica (formerly American Can), Navistar (formerly International Harvester), and Nissan (formerly Datsun). Sometimes the reasons include the following:

1.  The character of the business has changed, through acquisition and divestiture, so that the old name does not adequately represent the company.
2.  The "image" of the old name is not inkeeping with the corporate strategies of present management.

3.  There is perceived misunderstanding about the nature of the business among stockholders, investors, and investment analysts due to the name.

When these conditions are perceived, management can view an outmoded trademark as a hindrance. The legendary ad-man David Ogilvy has this to say:

> Whatever you do, for goodness sake, don't change the name of your corporation to *initials*. Everybody knows what IBM, ITT, CBS and NBC are, but how many of the following can *you* identify: AC . . . DHL . . . JVC . . . UBS. Yet this is how 37 corporations sign their advertisements. It will take them many years and many millions of dollars to teach their initials to their publics. What a waste of money.[10]

In support of Ogilvy, a survey regarding a few company name changes concluded:

> It's official: people hate the name Allegis. Also Unisys, Navistar, Primerica, NYNEX, USX and just about any other corporate name that sounds like it was cooked up by a NASA computer.[11]

Times change, companies change, and trademarks sometimes change with them. The essential point however, is, that trademarks are important to a business enterprise and are becoming ever more important. Like all intellectual property, trademarks are created and developed by human effort and human reaction. It is becoming ever more costly to create and develop well known trademarks. They have all the characteristics of becoming "collector's items," a form of art in short supply. In a somewhat less controversial mood, Ogilvy in 1983 said:

> It has become prohibitively expensive to launch brands aimed at a dominant share-of-market . . . The recent launch of a new cigarette cost $100,000,000 . . . There may never be another universal giant like Tide or Maxwell House.[12]

---

[10] David Ogilvy, *Ogilvy on Advertising*, Vintage Books, New York, 1983, p. 121.
[11] See footnote 10.
[12] David Ogilvy, *Ogilvy on Advertising*, Vintage Books, New York, 1983, p. 121.

The words of David Ogilvy have tremendous implications for investing in companies that possess well known trademarks. The *giants* that exist are rare and valuable. Companies that own these trademarks are in strong positions of economic advantage.

## Copyrights

A copyright protects the *expression* of an idea, not the idea itself. Copyright protection commences from the time when that expression is fixed in some tangible form, even prior to its publication. Formal applications to government agencies are not required. In fact, full copyright protection is present whether or not the work is registered with the Copyright Office of the Library of Congress.

A copyright owner may reprint, sell, or otherwise distribute the copyrighted work, prepare works that are derived from it, and assign, sell, or license it. If the author of a work created it as an adjunct to his or her employment, then a resulting copyright would be the property of the employer.

Copyrights are protected for a period of the life of the author plus 50 years. Title 17 of the United States Code defines a copyright as follows (Section 102):

> Copyright protection subsists . . . in original works of authorship fixed in any tangible medium of expression, now known or later developed, from which they can be perceived, reproduced, or otherwise communicated, either directly or with the aid of a machine or device. Included are:

1.  literary works;
2.  musical works, including any accompanying words;
3.  dramatic works, including any accompanying music;
4.  pantomimes and choreographic works;
5.  pictorial, graphic, and sculptural works;
6.  motion pictures and other audiovisual works;
7.  sound recordings.

An unpublished work may be registered by the following means:

1. Reducing the work to tangible form.
2. Transmitting an application form to the Copyright Office.
3. Transmitting a copy of the work and the registration fee to the Copyright Office.

A work to be published is protected by:

1. Publishing with the appropriate identifying marks.
2. Following steps 2 and 3 above, but furnishing *two* copies.

Because many copyrighted works such as films and recorded music are intended for wide distribution that is not easily controlled, the Copyright Royalty Tribunal was established to "make determinations as to reasonable terms and rates of royalty payments"(17 USC Section 801) for the use of such copyrighted works. The Register of Copyrights acts to distribute the royalties to the copyright owners of non dramatic musical works. These fees are collected from those, such as record companies, who distribute the works under license.

Really Useful Group is a company that consists of copyrights on the musicals of Andrew Lloyd Weber—*Cats, Phantom of the Opera,* and others. It has no manufacturing assets and little else in the way of traditional business enterprise assets. Yet the company is worth approximately $300 million.

## Computer Software and Copyrights

Revenue Procedure 69-21 (1969-2 CB 303) defines computer software to include:

> . . . all programs or routines used to cause a computer to perform a desired task or set of tasks, and the documentation required to describe and maintain those programs. Computer programs of all classes, for example, operating systems, executive systems, monitors, compilers and translators, assembly routines, and utility programs as well as application programs are included. Computer software does not include procedures which are external to the computer operations, such asinstructions to transcription operators and external control procedures.

The Copyright Act (17 USC Section 101) defines a computer program as:

. . . a set of statements or instructions to be used directly or indirectly in a computer in order to bring about a certain result.

This form of intellectual property can be extremely important to a business enterprise. The product is the software. It can be individual, stand-alone programs, or more complex modular systems that interface with one another, such as a general ledger system. The software may be sold with or without consultant support and related services.

Microsoft *(Windows)*, Lotus Development Corporation *(Lotus 1-2-3)*, First Generation Systems *(FastBack)*, and The Software Toolworks *(ChessMaster)* are only a few companies where the most important asset owned is software. Every corporate plan, strategy, and action undertaken is based on creating and selling small pieces of magnetized film that are laced with memory bits. All working capital and tangible assets exist to support the creation and sale of software. All other aspects of the corporate investment are subordinate.

One small software company had a gourmet kitchen as one of its most expensive tangible assets. The rest of the assets were comprised of standard personal computers that were used by programmers to create software products along with extra disk drive systems that were used to copy the programs. Other than the warehouse department, where disks were packaged for shipping, software was the primary asset of a company that was worth about $50 million. The special kitchen was worth almost $1 million. It was used to serve customized meals, 24 hours a day, to the stable of genius programmers. The rest of the tangible assets cost the company $3 million. The software products represented the remaining $46 million of company value.

---

### Key Investment Concept #7

Purchasing the stock of a software company is nothing more than purchasing a share in the software.

---

Computer programs can be patented if they embody computations that are carried out as part of a process claim or if they do more than just make mathematical calculations, and if they meet the other requirements of patentable material. Relatively few computer programs fall into this category.

Copyright protection is much more easily obtained. Remember that a copyright protects the *manner* of expression of an idea, however, it is very possible that a program can be developed to accomplish the same task as the protected one and, as long as the structure and sequence of the coding is not copied, the competing product does not infringe. The Copyright Office recently ruled that copyright protection extends to computer-screen displays, both graphic and text.

The courts of the United States, as well as those of Japan, West Germany, and France, are currently focused on the practical application of "idea" protection versus "expression" protection for software. Computer software is a unique form of communication that refuses to settle neatly into either patent or copyright statutes. The problem is to legally define the rights that attach to this form of intellectual property so as to protect authorship but not stifle further development. The next few years should see some landmark decision-making. At this time, the degree of protection available for software is unclear.

## Favorable Contracts

Two categories of favorable contracts exist where economic advantage is provided to the degree that an intangible asset comes into existence. The first involves source contracts. These contracts represent a means by which raw materials, labor or capital are obtained at an advantageous price. The second category involves output contracts where the company has a contract to deliver finished goods or services.

*Source Contracts*    Whenever a company can obtain one or more of the inputs of production on favorable terms above-average profits are not far behind. Just as a patented process can save manufacturing costs and thereby place the company in a position of competitive advantage, a favorable contract can enhance the competitive position of a company. Examples of favorable source contracts include the following:

1. The availability of long-term debt for the company at interest rates that are below market rates charged elsewhere. Often, the source of the funds are government agencies that are attempting to encourage investment in certain geographical locales or among "handicapped" ethnic groups.
2. Raw material contracts that will provide the company with scarce resources for a specified period of time.
3. Labor contracts that give the company an advantage over competitors.

Whenever a favorable source contract appears to exist, careful investigation is needed. For the most part, these contracts have specified expiration dates after which the favorable terms may not be renewable. High profit margins derived during the period of economic advantage may not continue after the expiration period. Investment decisions should be based on the period of time over which an advantage is enjoyed and the profit levels that are expected after the contract terminates. Funding from government agencies eventually will have to be replaced with conventional financing. Labor contracts come up for renewal and raw material prices may rise substantially at renegotiations.

---

Key Investment Concept #8

Favorable source contracts usually provide economic benefits that quickly terminate. The high profit margins enjoyed during the contract period may be artificial and after contract termination elusive.

---

*Output Contracts*    Agreements to purchase the goods and services of a company can be looked on as a favorable contract. Many defense contractors such as Lockheed, Northrop, and Grumman live for the existence of these contracts. In the airline industry, Boeing is an example of a company that regularly announces aircraft orders that have just been signed with airlines around the world. Economic advantages are derived from the synergistic planning that can be implemented. Once again, however, the contracts have a termination date that coincides with completion of the project. Worse, many of the contracts include cancellation clauses. The Peace Dividend that the Western world is hoping to enjoy has already hit defense contractors as the Defense Department revises downward many of its previously negotiated buying contracts. Cancellation clauses usually require a penalty payment but rarely is the amount enough to make up for the loss of long-term profits.

Output contracts are often cited as strong reasons to invest in a particular stock. The efficient market for goods that prevails in any capitalistic system, however, makes pricing of even long-term output contracts a competitive arrangement. In fact, many output contracts may hurt a company as the costs to satisfy the contract requirements exceed the costs that were anticipated at the signing of the agreement. Output contracts can often turn out to be negative intangible assets.

## Customer Relationships

Every business has customers, but not every business has customer relationships in the sense that they represent an intangible asset. In order for there to be a customer relationship in the sense of a valuable asset, there must be some obligation or advantage on the part of either the business or customer to continue the relationship. These factors create some "inertia," which tends to maintain the relationship, even when there is no contractual agreement between the parties. A loyal contingent of customers that patronize a company regularly represents a continuing base of business and relatively stable earnings.

Some examples of valuable customer relationships include the following:

1.  *Banking customers* who maintain deposits at a financial institution. The stable base of deposits represents the life blood of a bank's source of funds.

2. *Subscribers* to magazines, newspapers, and other periodicals. The demographics of the subscribers to *The Wall Street Journal* are the foundation on which the paper sets its rather impressive advertising rates. Without the subscriber base, ad rates for *The Wall Street Journal* could not be maintained.

3. *Parts customers* of an original equipment manufacturer regularly purchase after-market accessories and spare parts. In fact, some defense contractors produce original equipment in the form of tanks, fighter jets, and artillery at a break-even amount, knowing that an annuity of spare parts will run for the life of the equipment.

4. *Insurance policy holders* for fire, casualty, health, and life represent a steady flow of funds. Insurance companies make a significant amount of their profits from investment of the annual premiums that they collect. The funds can reliably be anticipated. Actuarial studies pinpoint the amounts that will likely be paid on claims with the rest of the inflow available for investment.

A stable of loyal customers with an incentive to stay with the company is a very valuable intangible asset. Changeover costs for many customers might be so great that a disaster is needed to motivate the customer to switch loyalties. A company that relies on IBM for all mainframe computers cannot quickly decide to change to DEC computers. With all the customer's EDP personnel trained to use the IBM equipment, a significant training investment would be lost with the decision to switch. Software investment in the millions of dollars might also be lost if they are unique to the IBM equipment. Quite often, customer relationships are well cemented even though a formal contract does not exist to tie the parties together.

## Distribution Networks

A business that depends on others to distribute and/or sell its products has relationships of considerable value. There are companies that sell cosmetics, cookware, and cleaning products in the residential market through representatives. These companies have no retail stores and the relationship with their representatives is extremely important.

Other businesses may sell complex products in a highly technical market through "manufacturers representatives." While there may be a contract between the company and its representatives, it is usually one that can be terminated on short notice and therefore does not itself ensure a continuation of the relationship. Locating, hiring, training, and maintaining such representation can be a very costly process and, once accomplished, the relationship is an asset of value to the enterprise.

It is important to note that, in this situation, the relationship between representative and customer may be stronger than the relationship between company and customer. Therefore the company–representative relationship may be very crucial to the welfare of the business.

## Intangible Life

The economic advantages derived from intangible assets do not last forever. Computer software products constantly face new competitive products that run faster, better, and at cheaper prices. Patented processes may have legal lives that run for 17 years but innovative competitors can often surpass current technologies with greater advances. Copyrights are unique but still face competition from new works and can fall victim to changing tastes and the fickle demand for classic literature, television reruns, and the song of our youth.

Customer relationships also change over time. Newspaper subscribers move, insurance policyholders die, and bank depositors withdraw savings to make purchases.

Listed in Exhibit 3-3 are general indications of the average remaining economic life of selected intangible assets. Economic life is the time period over which the intangible asset is expected to contribute to enhanced profits.

The financial performance of intangible asset investments are directly linked to the life of the asset and the firm's ability to either rejuvenate or develop replacement assets. Chapter 7 elaborates on the fragile nature of intangible asset magic.

*Exhibit 3-3*    Economic Life

| Intangible Asset | Economic Life |
| --- | --- |
| Personal computer software | 1–2 years |
| Computer mainframe hardware | 3–5 |
| Specialty adhesives formulas | 5–7 |
| Copyrighted college textbooks | 3–5 |
| Bank deposits | 5–7 |
| Pharmaceuticals | 10–17 |
| Newspaper advertisers | 5–7 |
| Industrial products customer base | 12–15 |
| Consumer product trademark | Unlimited |
| Copyrighted cartoon character | Unlimited |

## Goodwill

Goodwill is typically referred to as an intangible asset but does not really represent an independent intangible asset. Goodwill is the integrated benefit that is derived from the existence of intangible assets.

The idea of goodwill appears to have existed long before the advent of modern business concepts. P. D. Leake mentions some early references to goodwill, including one in the year 1571 in England, "I gyve to John Stephen . . . my whole interest and good will of my Quarrell" (i.e., quarry).[13]

In the simpler business organizations of [an] earlier period, goodwill was often of a rather personal nature, attaching in large measure to the particular personality, friendliness, and skill of the proprietor or partners of a business . . . As the industrial system developed and business increased in complexity, the various advantages which a business possessed and which contributed to its profitability became less personal in nature. The individual advantages which a company enjoyed became more varied, were integrated with all facets and activities of a business, and thus became less distinguishable. Manufacturing

---

[13] American Institute of Certified Public Accountants, *Accounting for Goodwill,* Accounting Research Study No.10, Stamford, CT, 1968, p. 8.

processes, financial connections, and technological advantages all assumed increasing importance. Goodwill came to be regarded as everything that might contribute to the advantage which an established business possessed over a business to be started anew.[14]

The situation for major corporations is a little more complex. It is largely an aggregation of recognizable intangible assets and intellectual property. Tearney finds that "the term 'goodwill' is an old term that has outlived its usefulness."[15]

Many equate goodwill with patronage or the proclivity of customers to return to a business and recommend it to others. This results from superior service, well regarded trademarks, product performance, advertising programs, or business policies that meet with favor in the marketplace. Individually, these are discreet intangible assets. Goodwill is the result of possessing valuable intangible assets but it isn't an independent asset.

Too often, high profit margins are vaguely attributed to a company's *goodwill*. Investment advisors that recommend a stock because the company has "tremendous goodwill" are doing investors a disservice because the advisors obviously do not understand the specific intangible asset that is truly the source of the above-average profits. Acceptance of "goodwill" as the basis for profits is overly simplistic and lazy. Premium selling prices are paid for patent product characteristics or well regarded trademarks. Long-term customer relationships may be established contractually or cemented by change-over costs. High profits may come from exclusive rights to distribute copyrights. Special trade secret formulas can also keep customers coming back for more and keep the cash flow of the company high. "Goodwill" has nothing to do with it. Specific intangible assets are the source of profits—not goodwill. Goodwill also wrongly infers an unlimited economic life for the high profits that are associated with the goodwill, but it just isn't so. Specific intangible assets have limited lives and can be supplanted by new inventions.

---

[14] See footnote 13, p.10.
[15] Michael G. Tearney, "Accounting for Goodwill: A Realistic Approach," *The Journal of Accountancy*, July 1973, p. 43.

## Franchise

Like goodwill the term *franchise* is bandied about and too quickly accepted as the source of superior company performance. One security analysis defines franchise as "the brand name and all that it stands for." Like using the term etc. at the end of a list, the author of this definition just doesn't understand the many categories of intangible assets that comprise a company. The term is often used as a smokescreen to mask a lack of real understanding about company fundamentals.

Traditionally, the term franchise is used in the context of owning one or more exclusive locations of McDonald's, Jiffy Lube, Mail Plus, Sir Speedy, or Midas Muffler. A specific geographic territory is conveyed in a legal agreement where the franchisee may operate the business. High profits have come to be associated with many of these ventures and the term franchise has taken on some of the connotations of the term monopoly. Transference of the term to companies with well regarded trademarks and exclusive cachet has unfortunately occurred. In reality, the assets that are truly involved with generating the superior profits include the trademarks, distribution networks, shelf space, advertising programs, customer perceptions, patented product characteristics, and special manufacturing techniques.

---

Key Investment Concept #9

Goodwill and franchise say nothing about the unique intangible assets that drive high profits. Thorough fundamental analysis requires a more detailed investigation.

---

## Loan Collateral and Liquidation

A new status has recently been attained by intangible assets. Major banks are considering the value of these items as loan collateral. Patents, trademarks, and copyrights are the trail blazers in this category. Even when a firm falls into bankruptcy, some of the intangible assets can have a residual or liquidation value. Drexel Burnham Lambert skyrocketed to become a leading Wall Street investment banker on the tailcoats of junk bonds. The fall from grace that was brought about by the insider trading scandal finished the firm. Still possessing value, however, was the firm's client list. To satisfy creditors, the firm put a database of 4000 names and contacts on the market. In addition, the following other intangible assets were put on the auction block:

Technical and pricing information on all the firm's public securities.

Technical and pricing information on all the firm's past merger and acquisition deals.

The firm's system for trading, selling, and researching high-risk, high-yield bonds (affectionately referred to as junk bonds).

Competitors could find this information extremely useful while trying to step into the void that was left by Drexel. Some of the information includes analytical software that Drexel developed for pricing M&A deals along with transaction information about thinly traded junk bonds.

The contact list could be the most appealing item up for sale. A list of decision-makers at corporations and investment firms showing who has been interested in risky financings. This could be a powerful tool for any firm desiring to enter or broaden their market.

The ultimate price paid for such information is dependent on the outlook for the future demand of junk bonds. So far, the 1990s have been characterized by saner merger and acquisition pricing with more respect given to the dangers of overleveraging. Still, the information may have value in the hands of the remaining Wall Street investment banks.

While this is an interesting development, investors should not place a great deal of reliance on the possible liquidation value of intangible assets when selecting stocks. If a business fails, liquidation of working capital components, tangible property, and the intellectual property may leave a residual amount after satisfying the lenders. Undoubtedly, however, the residual will not equal the initial investment. When considering an investment in a financially weak company with prospects for a turnaround, the focus should be placed on the potential for success and the reasonableness of the planned strategy.

---

### Key Investment Concept #10

Reliance on the liquidation value of intangible assets is not a compelling reason to invest in turnaround situations.

---

Intangible assets are fundamental to successful company performance. Without these assets, machinery remains idle in the plant and employees wander aimlessly in the parking lot. Surprisingly, the financial reports of companies carry very little information about intangible assets. In Chapter 9 the deficiencies of accounting statements and financial reports are explained.

In the next chapter, superior profits are linked to the existence of proprietary technology and contrasted with the poor economic performance margins associated with companies that lack this intangible asset.

# 4

# WHERE DO EARNINGS REALLY COME FROM?

Fully expanded, this chapter title is really asking the question . . . Where do the earnings that represent growth, high profitability, and a quickly appreciating stock price come from?

*The answer is found in the hidden intangible assets that we have been discussing.*

Intangible asset contributions to earnings are the primary force behind company value and the primary focus of this chapter. Theoretical background is first presented, followed by a detailed analysis of companies in the specialty chemicals industry. These companies are used to show the spectrum over which companies can benefit from possessing intangible assets.

Some of the material in this chapter is complex but the presentation has been structured to make this important material as painless as possible. Readers will be well rewarded for their efforts in reading this material. New insights about the fundamental source of corporate earnings lie just ahead.

## A Note About Earnings

Throughout this book a broad definition of earnings is used. Most recently, cash flow has been identified by academicians as the driving force behind stock prices.

Cash flow analysis is usually conducted in such a manner as to eliminate, wherever possible, some of the artful manipulations to net income that are used by creative and sometimes desperate company managements. Cash flow is becoming the preferred measure of economic benefits that are associated with valuing a stock. The use of the term *earnings* throughout this book is meant to describe, in broad terms, economic benefits that a company derives from its commercial activities. Earnings, as used here, are not used strictly to describe the accounting concept of net income.

Debt-free operating net income can be looked on as the total economic benefit that the business enterprise, and the assets of which it is comprised, generates from continuing operations. Absent from this measure of economic benefits are extraordinary items that are not expected to recur in the future. Unusual bad debt write-offs are an example, as are windfalls from large one-time-only contracts.

It is important to define the economic benefits produced by the enterprise on a debt-free basis to eliminate the interest expenses associated with debt. The economic benefits that are generated by the integrated assets are independent of the amount of debt used to finance the business. While some of the profits from the enterprise may be used to satisfy debt obligations, the contribution of the intangible assets must be studied unencumbered by debt. Interest expenses are associated with the financing decision of company management, which can substantially affect the overall company earnings. Debt ratios are a fundamental and important factor to analyze when studying investments but should be considered separately from the analysis of intangible asset contributions. Intangible asset contributions are independent of financial structures and should be studied in that manner.

In a comparison of two items of intangible assets, the property that generates sales, captures market share, and grows while using less selling and/or support efforts is more valuable than the one that requires extensive advertising, sales personnel, and administrative support. The economic benefits generated by the property are most accurately measured after considering all production, selling, and support efforts associated with the business.

---

Key Investment Concept #11

Compare the earnings contribution of intangible assets on a debt-free basis. Financial risks should be assessed separately.

---

## Intangible Assets Contribute Powerfully to Earnings

Delivering a product or service to customers involves costs. Rent, maintenance, utilities, salaries, raw materials, sales commissions, fees, and advertising are just some of the costs involved with delivering a product. When these costs are kept below the amount that customers pay for the product or service, a profit is earned.

The mere existence of profit, however, is not enough to justify company investments, nor is it a reason to buy stock in a company. Earnings derived from operations must be of an amount, on a consistent basis, to yield a fair rate of return on the investment over the term of the investment. A huge investment in fixed assets must be justified. Raw materials, industrial land, delivery trucks, manufacturing buildings, and production equipment cannot be justified if the funds that were used to buy and build these assets could generate a higher return from alternate investments. When T-bills produce an 8% return, a plant and equipment investment is expected to exceed 8% by an amount necessary to compensate for the added investment risk. In this chapter an analysis is presented that shows how intangible assets contribute to earnings and to company value by generating high profits using small amounts of fixed asset investment.

## Intangible Assets Can Beat an Efficient Economy

In our competitive economic environment, profits are eventually driven downward to the lowest level at which a fair return can still be extracted from participation in a mature market. Above-average profits are not often sustainable for long periods. Competitors are quick to recognize and enter high-profit markets. New entrants in a high-profit market force lower selling prices and squeeze profitability. This microeconomic process is efficient in general but can be bumpy for market participants along the way. Attractive profit levels often attract more competitors than the market will bear. When supply exceeds demand the corresponding reduction in selling prices can make the entire industry unprofitable for continued competition. After the inevitable shake-out the profitability of the industry tends toward the lowest price at which a fair return can still be earned. Previous glories of above-average profits become only memories.

---

Key Investment Concept #12

Look for companies that can consistently produce above-average profits and investment returns even in a mature market.

---

## Active Intangible Assets

When above-average profits are generated on a consistent basis, intangible assets are responsible. Active intangible assets are categorized as those that are directly responsible for generating a sustained amount of above-average profits. Active intangible assets work to control costs of production or introduce product characteristics that command premium selling prices. Sometimes intangible assets contribute by commanding a premium selling price on a consistent basis regardless of competitor actions. Well recognized trademarks are good examples. Two polo shirts of identical material and construction quality can differ in selling price by as much as $25.

Customers are willing to pay, on a consistent basis, more money for the Izod alligator. The same can be said to be true for other consumer goods like IBM personal computers, Sony televisions, Toro lawn mowers, Maytag kitchen appliances, and some of the Japanese automobile offerings. As long as the entire amount of premium isn't spent on image creating advertisements, net profits are enhanced.

Premium selling prices are not only associated with trademarks. Patented products can also command premium prices. An example is the ulcer drug, Tagamet. Generally, the production equipment investment that is needed to manufacture medicine tablets is similar to the equipment needed to make other medicines like aspirin. Patented drugs, however, are likely to sell at $1.00 or more per tablet while aspirin costs under 0.10 per tablet.

Production cost savings are another example where active intangible assets are a source of enhanced earnings. There are various ways that intangible assets can directly contribute to controlling production costs, including the following:

1.  Reduction in the amount of raw materials used.
2.  Substitution of lower cost materials without sacrifice of quality or product performance.
3.  Increases in the amount of production output per unit of labor input.
4.  Improved quality that reduces product recalls.
5.  Reduced use of electricity and other utilities.
6.  Production methods that control the amount of wear and tear on machinery and thereby reduce the amount of maintenance costs and production down-time for repairs.
7.  Elimination of manufacturing steps and the machinery investment previously used in the eliminated process.

When above-average profits are earned on a consistent basis, some form of intangible asset is responsible. Exhibit 4-1 illustrates this idea.

The middle bar represents the standard profitability for a product that is associated with a mature market that has completed the

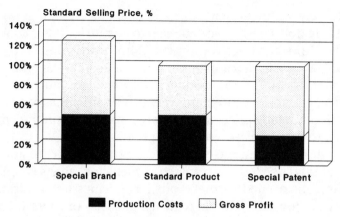

*Exhibit 4-1*    Intangible Asset Basic Contributions

shake-out phase of efficiency. The selling price is competitively determined in a mature industry at such a level that the market participants earn a fair rate of return on their investment, but sustained profits at an above-average level are no longer available to the typical competitor. Costs of production are shown at a hypothetical 50% of the selling price. The remaining 50% represents gross profits. The amount of gross profit that remains after paying for all other operating expenses represents net profits. In a mature market, net profits, after paying income taxes, are typically 4% of sales, or less.

The bar on the right shows the enhanced gross profitability that might be contributed by a patented process. Excluding use of the process by competitors allows the company to sell at the market price and enjoy higher profits due to production cost savings. Net profits are enhanced by the exact amount saved in production. Production costs in this example are reduced from the standard 50% of the selling price to 35%. The 15% savings translate to an *additional* 9% of sales after paying a tax rate of 40%. The total profit increases from 4% of sales to 13%.

The bar on the left shows a product that can consistently command a higher selling price. Production costs are the same, but the higher selling price allows enjoyment once again of above-average profits. The 25% premium price translates to an *additional* after-tax profit of 15%. Total profits increase to 19%. This example might be associated with a product that has a well regarded trademark for which people are willing to pay the premium price shown. In Chapter 5 this phenomenon is described in detail.

A combination of the two forces is also quite possible. A combination of intangible assets can provide a premium price and allow lower production costs, producing a compounding of enhanced earnings.

For illustrative purposes the amount of pricing premium and production cost savings has been exaggerated. Enhancements of only 1% or 2% can have dramatic earnings effects. A company with annual sales of $100 million can improve earnings by $2 million with a cost advantage or premium price. On an after-tax basis this can enhance earnings by 25%.

## Passive Intangible Assets

Enhanced profitability can also be derived from passive intangible assets. Profits aren't directly enhanced from premium selling prices or cost savings. These intangible assets can be just as valuable but their contribution to earnings enhancement is more subtle. Even when active contributions to earnings are not present, intangible assets can provide a company with above-average profits. A dominant position in a market allows a company to enjoy large amounts of sales volume on a consistent basis. Manufacturing and operating synergies can enhance profits. Only because of the passive intangible assets, however, is this possible.

Exhibit 4-2 represents the contribution of passive intangible assets as a collection of synergies that permeate through various functions of the company organization.

When large and reliable amounts of production volume consistently go through an organization, synergistic advantages are possible:

o Raw materials can be purchased at large-order discounts. Suppliers are likely to offer discounts to customers that place large orders. A cost savings is the result.

o Manufacturing efficiencies can be introduced throughout each step of the process.

FUNCTION

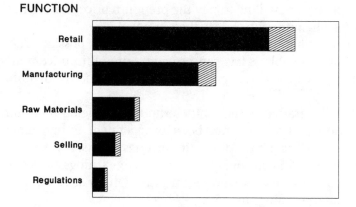

INTANGIBLE ASSET CONTRIBUTION TO VALUE

*Exhibit 4-2*   Intangible Asset Contribution to Company Value

- Selling expenses might be more controllable with fewer sales people covering large accounts.
- Retail efficiencies can include special arrangements with distributors or discounts in the purchase of shelf space at retailers.
- Regulation and compliance costs can be spread over a larger production base along with other fixed overhead costs.

Each synergistic benefit combines to provide enhanced profits, which is made possible by market-dominating intangible assets like trademarks and distribution networks.

---

Key Investment Concept #13

Superior profits and investment returns can be derived from both active and passive intangible assets. The best investment opportunities enjoy economic benefits from a combination of both types of intangible assets.

---

## Intangible Asset Contributions to Company Value

Presented in the remainder of this chapter is an analysis that compares the performance of companies with intangible assets to those that are stuck in a mediocre commodity business. Companies in the specialty chemicals business are analyzed for this comparison. The analysis focuses on the earnings that are attributed to the existence of intangible assets. From this analysis, key characteristics of companies that possess valuable intangible assets are identified and listed for use in finding winning stocks.

*Intangible assets rarely generate economic benefits alone.* Rather, complementary assets, in the form of working capital and tangible assets, are typically combined into a business enterprise. This *portfolio* of assets generates an overall economic return. Allocation of the company returns among the asset categories that comprise the *portfolio* can isolate the amount of return that is attributable to the intangible assets.

## How Much Did the Intangible Assets Earn?

Isolating the stream of economic benefits that are derived from intangible assets is the key to ultimately defining and understanding the characteristics that successful intangible asset companies possess. The required analysis allocates the economic benefits from the overall business enterprise to the asset categories that are employed in the generation of these benefits.

The allocation must address two important factors:

1. The relative amount of each asset category involved in the business.
2. The appropriate rate of return to associate with each asset category.

Business enterprises are comprised of monetary assets, tangible assets, and intangible assets. Economic benefits are generated from the integrated employment of these complementary assets—that is, net profits. Each asset contributes. Based on the relative importance of each asset category and the risk associated with each asset category, the aggregate income of the enterprise can be allocated to its components.

The process of allocating the debt-free operating net income among the assets of the business enterprise focuses on the value of the assets in each category and an appropriate rate of return on each. Composition of a business enterprise basically consists of the following:

- *Monetary assets*, in the form of net working capital
- *Tangible assets*, as represented by buildings and machinery
- *Intangible assets*, which include intellectual property such as patents and trademarks

Each of these asset categories contributes to the overall achievement of debt-free operating net income.

Before it is possible to allocate the enterprise debt-free operating net income, we must first determine an appropriate rate of return to associate with each of the component parts. Starting with the rate of return requirement for the overall enterprise, we can estimate the rates of return for each asset category.

## Rate of Return Requirements from the Integrated Portfolio of Business Assets

Corporate investments typically must pass hurdle rates in order to be considered as viable opportunities. Since debt and equity funds are used to finance these investments, the return that is provided must be sufficient to satisfy the interest due on the debt and also provide a fair rate of return on the equity funds. The hurdle rate must be the weighted average cost of capital, at a minimum, in order to earn a fair rate of return on invested capital. The cost to the company of the invested capital equals the rate of return that the investors expect to receive less any tax benefits that the company enjoys, such as the deductibility of interest expenses.

The invested capital was previously defined as the summation of equity funds and debt obligations. These total funds were then used to obtain or create the complementary assets of the business, including land, buildings, machinery, truck fleets, office equipment, patented technology, and net working capital.

Airgas, Inc. is one of the specialty chemicals companies contained in the analysis to be presented. Its weighted average cost of capital (WACOC) is presented in Exhibit 4-3.

The tax deductibility of interest expense makes the after-tax cost of debt only 54% of the stated interest rate for the corporation. Airgas pays a combined state and federal income tax of 46%. Equity returns are in no way tax deductible. When the costs of these capital components are weighted by their percentage of the total capital structure, a weighted average cost of capital of 14.3% is the result. This is the amount of return that the company must earn on its overall investment as comprised of the monetary, tangible, and intangible assets. Each asset component must provide a portion of the overall return *relative to the risk associated with that asset.*

The weighted average cost of capital requirement can be allocated among the assets that are employed within the business enterprise. The allocation is conducted with respect to the amount of investment risk that each component represents to the business enterprise. Just as the weighted average cost of capital is allocated among the debt and equity components of the invested capital, it is also possible to allocate a portion of the WACOC to the asset components with consideration given to the relative risk associated with each category of assets.

*Exhibit 4-3*   Airgas, Inc. Weighted Cost of Capital

| Invested Capital Component | Amount ($ Millions) | Percentage of Invested Capital | Cost of Capital | After-tax Cost of Capital | Weighted Average Cost of Capital |
|---|---|---|---|---|---|
| *Equity* | 116.2 | 37.4% | 26.1% | 26.1% | 9.8% |
| *Debt* | 194.6 | 62.6% | 13.5% | 7.3% | 4.6% |
| *Total* | 310.8 | 100.0% | | | 14.3% |

## Appropriate Return on Monetary Assets

The monetary assets of the business are its net working capital. This is the total of current assets minus current liabilities. Current assets are comprised of accounts receivable, inventories, cash, and short-term security investments. Offsetting this total are the current liabilities of the business, such as accounts payable, accrued salaries, and accrued expenses.

Working capital is considered to be the most liquid asset of a business. Receivables are usually collected within 60 days and inventories are sometimes turned over in 90 days. The cash component is immediately available and security holdings can be converted to cash with a telephone call to the firm's broker. Further evidence of liquidity is the use of accounts receivable and/or inventories as collateral for loans. In addition, accounts receivable can be sold for immediate cash to factoring companies at a discount of the book value.

Given the relative liquidity of working capital, the amount of investment risk is inherently low in comparison to that of the other asset categories. An appropriate rate of return to associate with the working capital component of the business enterprise is typically lower than the overall WACOC. A surrogate rate of return can be used to estimate a proper amount to associate with the working capital—that which is available from investment in short-term securities of low-risk levels. The rate available on 90 day certificates of deposit or money market funds can serve as a benchmark. While net working capital may be more risky than bank deposits, it is still much less risky than the other asset categories.

A corporation, as an alternative, could earn a low-risk, short-term rate of return on working capital if it were not invested in the operating business. As such, the operations of the business must earn at least that amount on working capital.

## Appropriate Return on Tangible Assets

Tangible or fixed assets of the business are comprised of production machinery, warehouse equipment, transportation fleet, office buildings, office equipment, leasehold improvements, and manufacturing plants.

While these assets are not as liquid as working capital, they still possess some elements of marketability. They can often be sold to other companies or used for alternate commercial purposes. This marketability allows a partial return of the investment in fixed assets of the business should the business fail.

Another aspect of relative risk reduction relates to the strategic redeployment of fixed assets. Assets that can be redirected for use elsewhere in a corporation have a degree of versatility which can still allow an economic contribution to be derived from their employment even if it isn't from the originally intended purpose.

While these assets are more risky than working capital investments, they possess favorable characteristics that must be considered in the weighted average cost of capital allocation. An indication of the rate of return that is contributed by these assets can be pegged at about the interest rate at which commercial banks make loans, using the fixed assets as collateral. Use of these rates must be adjusted, however, to reflect the equity risk position of the owners, which is slightly riskier than that of lenders.

Fixed assets that are very specialized in nature must reflect higher levels of risk, which of course demands a higher rate of return. Specialized assets are those that are not easily redeployed for other commercial exploitation or liquidated to other businesses for other uses. They may be closely tied to the intangible assets and possess little chance for redeployment. In this case, a rate of return similar to that required on intangible assets may be more appropriate. In general, the tangible assets of a business are less risky than the intangible assets.

An alternative fixed asset investment for a company could be capital leasing of fixed assets to other manufacturers, where it would earn a return commensurate with the risk of collateralized lending. When an operating business is chosen as the investment vehicle, then, as a minimum, the collateralized lending rate of return must be earned on the fixed assets that are used.

## Appropriate Return on Intangible Assets

Since intangible value is often subject to more radical fluctuations than is tangible value (if the business deteriorates the tangible assets will likely continue to have some value in the marketplace whereas the intangible value may quickly disappear), the intangible assets of a business are at greater risk than are the tangible assets.

Intangible assets are considered to be the most risky asset components of the overall business enterprise. Trademarks can get out of sync with the attitudes of society and patents can be made obsolete by advancing technology of competitors. Until recently, the Keds sneaker brand name was associated with unsophisticated nerds. Its fragile nature with regard to consumer attitudes makes it and other forms of intangible assets risky properties to own. As such, a higher rate of return, relative to the other complementary assets, is required. These assets may have little, if any, liquidity and poor versatility for redeployment elsewhere in the business. This increases their risk. Customized computer software that is installed and running on a company's computer may have very little liquidation value if the company fails. The investment in a trained workforce may be altogether lost and the value of other elements of a going concern is directly related to the success of the business. A higher rate of return on these assets is therefore required. Since the overall return on the business is established as the weighted average cost of capital and since reasonable returns for the monetary and tangible assets can be estimated, we are then in a position to derive an appropriate rate of return to be earned by the intangible assets.

## Allocation of the WACOC

Airgas, Inc. has a total value of invested capital of $310.8 million as shown in Exhibit 4-4.

Equity value is calculated as the number of shares outstanding multiplied by the price per share of $16.75. Debt has been valued for this example using the book value presented in the financial

*Exhibit 4-4*    Airgas Inc. Invested Capital Value ($ Millions)

| | |
|---|---|
| Common Shareholders' Equity | $116.2 |
| Preferred Shareholders' Equity | 0.0 |
| Long-Term Debt Obligations | 194.6 |
| Total Value of Invested Capital | $310.8 |

Exhibit 4-5    Airgas, Inc. Asset Category Values

|  | Value ($ Million) | Percentage of Total |
|---|---|---|
| *Working Capital* | 53.1 | 17.1% |
| *Fixed Assets* | 133.2 | 42.8% |
| *Subsidiary Investments* | 59.0 | 16.0% |
| *Intangible Assets* | 65.5 | 20.0% |
| Total | 310.8 | 100.0% |

statements of the company. During times of volatile interest rates fluctuation adjustments to the debt value may be warranted.

Airgas, Inc. is comprised of various asset categories, which must equal the value of the invested capital: net working capital, fixed assets for manufacturing and distribution, other assets (investments in subsidiaries), and the intangible assets that are used in the business. Exhibit 4-5 balances the total amount of invested capital among all these assets.

The source of values for the allocation are shown in Exhibit 4-6.

Each of these assets contributes to the overall required rate of return. For Airgas, Inc. the required return was determined to be 14.3%. Based on the relative risk discussion presented earlier, Exhibit 4-7 assigns different levels of required return to the different asset categories.

As a result of these investment rate of return requirements, the intangible assets of Airgas account for almost 30% of the total debt-free operating net income of the company even though these same assets account for only 20% of the overall enterprise value. Of the $14.9 million of debt-free operating net income generated by the company recently, $4.4 million is attributed to the intangible assets.

Exhibit 4-6    Airgas, Inc. Source of Value

| Asset Category | Source of Value |
|---|---|
| *Net Working Capital* | Book value as reported in the company financial statements. |
| *Fixed Assets* | Average of the gross and net amounts shown in the financial statements. Net value is considered to understate the operating value of assets due to aggressive depreciation policies. |
| *Subsidiary Investments* | Book value from the financial statements. |
| *Intangible Assets* | Residual amount of invested capital after allocation to the other assets listed above. |

*Exhibit 4-7*    Airgas, Inc. Required Rate of Return Among Assets

| Asset Category | Amount ($ Millions) | Percent of Invested Capital | Return Required | Weighted Return Required | Percent of Total Return |
|---|---|---|---|---|---|
| Net Working Capital | 53.1 | 17.1% | 8.0% | 1.4% | 9.6% |
| Fixed Assets | 133.2 | 42.9% | 13.5% | 5.8% | 40.4% |
| Subsidiary Investments | 59.0 | 19.0% | 15.5% | 2.9% | 20.6% |
| Intangible Assets | 65.5 | 21.1% | 20.0% | 4.2% | 29.5% |
| Total | 310.8 | 100.0% | | 14.3% | 100.0% |

Without the existence of intangible assets, the company could be expected to have earned only about $10 million. *Excess returns were earned from the employment of intangible assets.* As a percentage of sales, the excess returns represent 1.5% of sales as shown in Exhibit 4-8.

Airgas, Inc. generated enough earnings to provide a fair rate of return on the complementary assets and to still have excess earnings generated from intangible assets. In comparison with other companies in the specialty chemicals industry, Airgas, Inc. shows paltry levels of excess returns.

Airgas, Inc. showed a low level of excess earnings, which isn't surprising. The company is a distributor of industrial gases in 28 states. As a distributor the primary assets of the company are inventory and distribution equipment. Intangible assets, if any, are comprised of loyal customers. The commodity nature of the product, however, connects customer loyalty primarily with low-cost sup-

*Exhibit 4-8*    Airgas, Inc. Intangible Asset Excess Return on Sales

| Asset Category | Amount ($ Millions) | Percent of Total Return | Allocation of the D F N I | as Percent of Sales |
|---|---|---|---|---|
| Net Working Capital | 53.1 | 9.6% | 1.4 | 0.5% |
| Fixed Assets | 133.2 | 40.4% | 6.0 | 2.0% |
| Subsidiary Investments | 59.0 | 20.6% | 3.1 | 1.0% |
| Intangible Assets | 65.5 | 29.5% | 4.4 | 1.5% |
| Total | 310.8 | 100.0% | 14.9 | 5.0% |

pliers. Premium pricing isn't an option for enhancing the profits of the company. Other companies in this analysis possess patented formulations, manufacturing know-how, and trade secrets—all of which contribute to the generation of excess earnings at a much higher level.

## Specialty Chemicals Intangible Assets

Companies in the specialty chemicals industry were all analyzed using the same technique just applied to Airgas, Inc. in a search for excess intangible asset returns. A total of 45 companies were analyzed. Presented in Exhibit 4-9 is a regression analysis of the results, showing the distribution pattern of the excess returns.

Along the bottom axis of the graph is plotted the amount of excess returns presented as a percentage of sales. Companies at the left side of the graph were unable to earn an excess return above the required rate expected on monetary and fixed assets. Some of the companies weren't even able to earn enough to cover the required rate of return on the monetary and fixed assets.

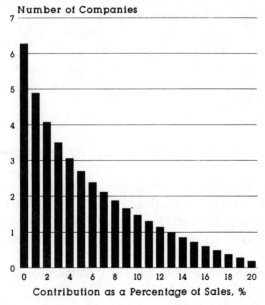

*Exhibit 4-9*   Specialty Chemicals & Synthetics: Contribution of Intangible Assets

In fact, seven of the companies analyzed (20% of the total) didn't earn enough profit to cover the monetary and fixed asset return requirements. These low rates of return are associated with semi-commodity businesses, such as industrial gas distribution. Companies earning an excess amount of return of 5% or less represented 50% of the entire group. Moving to the right of the graph, we find fewer and fewer companies earning increased excess returns. Less than 25% of the companies were able to earn more than 10% of sales as excess return.

Brights spots, however, exist where extraordinary amounts of excess profits were generated. After earning a fair rate of return on net working capital and fixed assets, a few of these companies earned as much as 20% of sales as above-average profits.

Trademarks are considered less important as part of the buying decision for specialty chemicals. While important to consumer goods, purity, quality, performance, and price are the hallmark of selling specialty chemicals. The excess returns of this industry are therefore attributed to technological know-how and patented products. Supporting information can be found by analysis of advertising expenses and R&D expenditures. While very little effort is placed behind advertising, R&D expenses in the specialty chemicals industry are substantial and growing. The industry is characterized as being in a *new materials renaissance*. Products include engineering polymers, composites, advanced ceramics, and improved adhesives. All require extensive R&D efforts yielding valuable technological know-how and excess earnings.

## Characteristics of Successful Intangible Asset Companies

High amounts of excess returns are associated with companies that earn a fair rate of return on their monetary and fixed assets with significant amounts left over. Technological know-how is considered to be the source. These companies have certain characteristics:

○ High amounts of sales for each dollar invested in working capital and fixed assets
○ High levels of gross profit

- High levels of operating income
- High returns on working capital and fixed asset investments
- High PE ratio valuations
- High market to book valuations

More revenues from less investment in fixed assets and working capital are a highly desirable characteristic of successful companies with intangible assets. Financial statements can provide the information needed for this analysis. Calculation of a *fixed turnover ratio* divides the total amount of sales by the value of net working capital (current assets less current liabilities) and the value of plant, property, and equipment (PP&E). For comparison purposes with other companies the gross value, or original cost, of the PP&E is better to use in order to avoid the distortions that can be associated with different depreciation policies (net book value of PP&E for two companies with identical equipment, purchased at the same price on the same date can be quite different, depending on the methods that are presented for depreciation). Technology that allows more production efficiencies can reduce the need to expand physical plant capacity. Less debt is needed to finance plant construction and the risk of being stuck with overcapacity during recessions is reduced.

High returns on the gross value of fixed assets is another indication that valuable intangible assets are part of company value. A desirable characteristic involves high earnings from less investment in plant facilities.

High levels of gross profit mean that cost savings are being enjoyed somewhere in the production process. A technology might be reducing the amount of raw materials used or might allow the substitution of lower cost materials. Utility usage may be reduced or labor-saving technology may be the source. Also, high levels of operating income indicate that the savings realized in the production of the product can be carried through to the bottom line.

For the most part, the balance sheets of these companies did not include a value classification for intangible assets. Only when intangible assets are acquired in third-party transactions are they represented on the balance sheet. Their absence indicates that, at least for the specialty chemicals industry, valuable intangible assets were developed in-house. This accounts for the high price-to-book value of equity ratios as a characteristic of companies with high levels of excess returns. The balance sheet may not show the intangible assets but the marketplace for these stocks recognizes that they exist and are valuable. As a result, the price of the common stock divided by the balance sheet amount shown as equity is a high ratio.

Investment styles that look for low price-to-book value ratios are too limiting when trying to identify companies that possess valuable intangible assets. Accounting for intangible assets is thoroughly addressed in a later chapter.

---

Key Investment Concept #14

Low price-to-book value of equity ratios should not be used as an improtant criterion when selecting stocks of companies with intangible assets.

---

High PE ratios (price of common stock divided by earnings) tend to be associated with successful intangible asset companies. This characteristic is associated with companies that have displayed fast earnings growth. When this is expected to continue, a high PE ratio is associated with the stock. While many investors look for *bargain* companies, as measured by low PE ratios, a more useful analysis is to focus on the reason for a high PE ratio. When fast earnings growth is expected to continue, investors shouldn't rule out purchasing intangible asset rich companies.

## Stock Performance Accompanies Intangible Assets

All this analysis isn't just for the fun of crunching numbers. Exhibit 4.10 shows that the companies with high levels of excess earnings provided by intangible asset also provided high returns for investors.

Investment returns were calculated as the compound rate of return from holding the stock of these companies for 10 years and included the amount of return that was provided by dividends.

| Company | Investment Return | Excess Return from Intangibles |
|---|---|---|
| Sigma–Alrich Corp | 27.6% | 12.0% |
| Flamemaster Corp | 22.1% | 7.2% |
| Great Lakes Chemical Corp | 18.6% | 16.3% |
| WD 40 Corp | 17.0% | 20.0% |
| Learonal Inc | 16.6% | 6.2% |
| Nalco Chemical Company | 16.4% | 8.8% |
| Loctite Corp | 15.0% | 11.5% |
| Lawter International Inc | 14.2% | 13.7% |
| Detrex Corp | 10.1% | 0.0% |
| MacDermid Inc | 9.7% | 1.5% |
| Kinark Corp | 9.5% | 2.2% |
| Lubrizol Corp | 6.4% | 6.0% |
| Petrolite Corp | 5.0% | 1.0% |
| Nuclear Metals Inc | –5.6% | 0.0% |
| Pacer Technology Corp | –16.4% | –1.6% |

*Exhibit 4-10*    Intangible Asset Companies Investment Rate of Return

Companies that didn't yield high levels of excess returns also didn't yield a reasonable rate of investment return. Companies with high excess earnings, for the most part, rewarded investors very nicely.

## Underutilized Intangible Assets

Initially, this technique was presented as a means by which valuable intangible assets could be identified. Additionally, it can be used to clearly identify intangibles that are underutilized.

If the allocation analysis is performed on a company that is known to possess intangible assets, like a well regarded trademark, it may turn out that the company is earning only enough to cover the required return on the monetary and fixed asset investment. Little or nothing might be left as a return on the well regarded intangibles. If

---

Key Investment Concept #15

Look for companies that are undermanaging their valuable intangible assets. These companies are excellent takeover candidates. They will be the focal point of acquisitions in the coming decade.

the intangibles are known to have intrinsic value, they may be undermanaged. A company that falls into this category would be a likely candidate for takeover.

### Long-Term Intangible Investing

Intangible assets do not grow on trees. They aren't available in local hardware stores and can't be "wished" into existence by ambitious managers. Development of technology involves extensive R&D efforts and keystone trademarks need years of advertising exposure. Investment patience is needed.

There is an unfortunate impression that stock prices are driven by next-quarter earnings. In reality, the market invests for the long term. This is easily proved by examining the current share price of a company's common stock relative to the expected amount of dividends that an investor can expect to receive. A random sample of Fortune 500 companies was analyzed in *Valuation,* by Copeland, Koller, and Murrin. Exhibit 4-11 shows that less than 12% of the stock price for the selected companies could be attributed to the amount of dividends that were expected to be received over the next 5 years. The majority of the value a company as represented by the stock price is therefore attributed to the investment results that are expected beyond that period.

A long-term investment perspective is especially true for companies that rely on intangible assets. When the management of a company announces a significant event will affect long-term earnings, stock prices react. A study of 120 company announcements, by the Securities and Exchange Commission, involving plans to increase R&D expenditures, was met by the market with stock price increases. While these added expenses will lower company earnings in the near term, the market recognizes that the new technologies and products that are likely to be developed will generate enhanced earnings over the long term. The announced R&D expenditures are expected to create valuable intangible assets and the stock prices react favorably. In Chapter 7 you will see that the market rewards continued financial support for maintaining trademarks and R&D efforts. An illuminating analysis shows a strong correlation between pharmaceutical patents and investor returns.

*Exhibit 4-11*   Present Value of Expected Dividends Versus Price for 20 Fortune 500 Companies, October 1988

| Company | Share price | Present value of dividends expected over next 5 yrs. | Dividends as percentage of stock price |
|---|---|---|---|
| Aluminum Company of America | $55 | $5.71 | 10.4% |
| Becton, Dickinson & Company | 57 | 3.91 | 6.9 |
| Bristol-Myers Company | 45 | 8.10 | 18.0 |
| Champion Spark Plug Company | 13 | 1.03 | 7.9 |
| Chesapeake Corp. | 21 | 2.21 | 10.5 |
| Coleman Company, Inc. | 37 | 5.17 | 14.0 |
| Esselte Business Systems, Inc. | 33 | 3.79 | 11.5 |
| Exxon Corporation | 45 | 8.95 | 19.9 |
| Fieldcrest Cannon, Inc. | 22 | 2.56 | 11.6 |
| Grumman Corp. | 22 | 4.16 | 18.9 |
| Jefferson Smurfit Corp. | 27 | 1.92 | 7.1 |
| Johnson Controls, Inc. | 35 | 4.35 | 12.4 |
| Lone Star Industries, Inc. | 32 | 6.58 | 20.6 |
| McDonnell Douglas Corporation | 72 | 11.25 | 15.6 |
| Medtronic, Inc. | 80 | 5.30 | 6.6 |
| Newmont Mining Corporation | 36 | 2.61 | 7.2 |
| Nucor Corp. | 42 | 1.82 | 4.3 |
| Reynolds Metals Company | 54 | 4.08 | 7.6 |
| Rohm and Haas Company | 34 | 4.25 | 12.5 |
| Westvaco Corp. | 30 | 3.59 | 12.0 |
| Average | | | 11.8% |

## Summary

Intangible assets in the form of trademarks and patents dramatically contribute to earnings. The return on monetary and fixed asset investments can be propelled to extraordinary levels with the introduction of intangible assets.

---

Key Investment Concept #16

Intangible assets are the most important possession of a company. They generate above-average profits and the stock market rewards investors that recognize their power.

---

# 5

# THE POWER OF TRADEMARKS

In 1989 the Top 100 national advertisers spent $32.2 billion on newspaper, magazine, television, radio, and billboard, advertising to create and maintain trademarks (source *Advertising Age*). The money wasn't spent just for the fun of it or to evade taxes. It was *invested* in valuable intangible assets—trademarks.

Trademarks are badges of identification and guarantees of quality for consumers. Trademarks command premium prices, represent customer loyalty, and sometimes dominate markets.

A trademark is a sign or a symbol that distinguishes the goods or services that are provided by an enterprise. The trademark has three functions:

1. To distinguish the goods or services from competitors.
2. To indicate the source of the goods or services.

3.  To represent the goodwill of the manufacturer and to serve as an indication of the quality of the product.

The power of trademarks is simply staggering. They conjure up images, work at both the conscious and subconscious levels, and cut across barriers of race, religion, and language. Symbols are universal and are recognized across the globe. Since the earliest time of commerce, goods have been marked to distinguish them from the products of competitors. The process first began with craftspeople placing a customized mark on unique designs and products.

Currently, most trademarks are associated with products that are relatively undifferentiated in terms of product specification, performance, and quality. Starting from the roots of innovation, trademarks derived their power from unique product characteristics and performance. Competitive products quickly emerged equaling all aspects of quality, price, and performance. Eventually, the only distinquishing characteristics remaining for customers became the trusted image and emotional comfort that comes from staying with an old friend.

Creating a trademark that possesses emotional characteristics requires a mountain of money in the form of advertising, but it also takes more. Establishing and maintaining a strong trademark requires the clear positioning of the trademark, with strict adherence to the image that is desired. In keeping with the trademark positioning, a strategy needs to be established, understood, and adhered to relentlessly. All aspects of the marketing strategy must conform, including the product, its packaging, pricing, distribution, and advertising campaign. It won't work to put an upscale product with expensive packaging in gas station convenience stores.

To complicate things further, the trademarks must maintain their image in an ever changing market because people's needs change, values change, and tastes evolve. The environment in which trademarks must operate is not static. Vigilant attention to the trademark image and its market position is the only way to keep the trademark valuable.

Continued advertising is a key component. In 1989 McDonald's spent $424.8 million on its trademark. This is the largest amount of money ever spent in a single year on a single trademark. Second place went to Kellogg's cereals with $373.3 million of spending.

Rewards were significant. Just look at the top ten trademarks as measured by the amount of advertising dollars in 1989. All are highly recognized in the United States and around the world.

Top Ten Advertising
for a Single Trademark

1. McDonald's
2. Kellogg's
3. Sears
4. AT&T
5. Ford
6. Budweiser
7. Chevrolet
8. Nissan
9. Burger King
10. Toyota

Advertising can provide the following benefits.

1. Creates a new trademark.
2. Nurtures and supports the image and position of a well established trademark.
3. Influences the behavior of consumers.
4. Enhances a corporate image.
5. Attracts bright employees.
6. Influences behavior with regard to purchasing of company stock.

Once established it's hard to beat down a well known trademark. Enormous amounts of money are needed by competitors.

Trademark benefits are primarily twofold. Quite often a premium price can be charged. Ralph Lauren can get almost $25 more for a cotton polo shirt because of the trademark. As long as the entire premium isn't spent on advertising, which is rarely the case, most of the higher price goes to the profit line.

The other benefit from a well known trademark is market dominance. Even when the premium pricing advantage is small, a dominant share of a market can provide synergistic benefits in manufacturing and administration. A company that controls 50% of the market is likely to be able to cut a better deal with raw material suppliers than the company with only 5% of the market.

## Competitive Barriers

The strength of existing trademarks is further enhanced by the obstacles that competitors face when trying to establish new and competing trademarks. In static industries that have matured, creating a new trademark requires a significant effort to turn the heads of loyal customers. Meanwhile, established companies are not likely to be idle as someone else approaches their turf. Established companies are likely to aggressively accelerate advertising and even provide price discounts to shift the attention back to the well known trademark.

It is also difficult for new competitors to be technologically differentiated. Product qualities are converging. Increasingly, products are at technological parity among the major manufacturers. It is becoming more difficult to introduce a revolutionary new product that can serve as the foundation for a new trademark.

Distribution outlets are unlikely to help a new competitor either. The influence of the retailer for many industries, especially food, is diverting much of the funds that are normally used for developing and positioning new trademarks to price promotions. Retailers are insisting that promotional activities such as coupon discounts take on more importance. Advertising dollars for establishing image and position are thus being drained. It is also difficult to convince store buyers to risk their careers by allocating limited floor space to new products that don't have an established following.

Marketing expenses are also growing as manufacturers respond to the escalating cost of reaching the consumer. Establishing a new trademark can be even more expensive than the billions spent to entrench the old-line names. The fragmentation of the maturing population is difficult to reach. With so many magazines, cable television channels, and expanding forms of media, it is difficult for advertisers to find a central location that will reach a large audience with a new trademark.

A well established trademark beckons loyal customers over to the store shelves. It also represents a huge obstacle to anyone interested in entering the market.

## Long-lasting Value

A book entitled *The Leadership of Advertised Brands,* published by Doubleday in 1923, contained a list of trademarks that had "mental dominance" with the consuming public at the time it was published. The trademarks listed in Exhibit 5-1 were mentioned twice as many times as the next trademark in the same field. The majority are still powerful juggernauts in their respective fields. Clearly, this list exemplifies the powerful and enduring nature of established trademarks. Many times the trademarks gained prominence by being pioneers in quality or product efficacy. Once dominant, dislodging a

*Exhibit 5-1*    Trademarks with "Mental Dominance" of the 1920s

| Trademark | Product Category |
|---|---|
| Ivory | Soap |
| Gold Medal | Flour |
| Coca-Cola | Soft drinks |
| B.V.D. | Underwear |
| Stetson | Hats |
| Kellogg's Corn Flakes | Breakfast food |
| Colgate | Dentifrice |
| Goodyear | Tires |
| Winchester | Guns |
| Hart Schaffner & Marks | Men's clothing |
| Ed Pinaud | Hair tonic |
| Steinway | Pianos |
| Ford | Automobiles |
| Arbuckle | Coffee |
| Heinz | Spaghetti |
| Del Monte | Canned fruits |
| Fels Naptha | Laundry soap |
| Djer Kiss | Face powder |
| Iver Johnson | Bicycles |
| Mazda | Lamps |
| Fleischer's | Yarns |
| Cross | Leather goods |

Exhibit 5-2    Trademarks from the 1890s

> American Express Travelers Checks
> Armour Beef Extract
> Dixons Pencils
> Heinz Baked Beans
> Hires Root Beer
> Ivory Soap
> Kodak
> Lipton Teas
> Mennen's Talcum Powder
> Prudential Insurance Company
> Quaker Oats
> Regal Shoes
> Sante Fe Railroad
> Sears Roebuck & Company
> Steinway Piano
> Van Camps Pork and Beans
> Waterman Fountain Pen
> Winchester Arms

reigning trademark takes considerable strategizing and financial backing in the form of advertising.

Another list also helps to demonstrate the extraordinarily long and successful lives that trademarks can enjoy. Listed in Exhibit 5-2 are trademarks that were well recognized in the United States in the 1890s.

The manufacturing buildings, product designs, packaging, office equipment, corporate strategies, and employees once associated with these grand names are long gone. Even the underlying product technology, patented or otherwise, hasn't lasted as long. The trademarks, however, are still vital and contributing to the success of their businesses. Of all the corporate assets that can be possessed, only trademarks have such longevity and power.

---

### Key Investment Concept #17

Trademarks are the most enduring assets that any corporation can hope to own.

---

## The Power to Differentiate

One way to make money in a commodity business is to buy an age-old trademark and attach it to your product. That is just what they did at Packard Bell.

The original Packard Bell name was associated with a company that made radios in the 1920s and television sets in the 1950s. Like many U.S. consumer electronics companies, foreign competition had a detrimental effect on the company. In 1968 Teledyne Corporation purchased Packard Bell, which by the mid 1970s was, for the most part, disbanded. A computer parts distributor named Beny Alagem purchased the name from Teledyne in 1985 for less than $100,000 and attached it to personal computers his company assembled in California. The combination of merchandising know-how, product quality, and the Packard Bell name has given the company approximately a 26% share of the billion dollar personal computer market, sold through warehouses, discount stores, electronic stores, and appliance centers. The sales for the company reached $600 million in 1989.

George Pursglove, vice president and general merchandise manager of HQ Office Supply Warehouse in Long Beach, California, was quoted by *Forbes* as saying: "buying that name was a stroke of genius . . . Older customers think Packard Bell is the company that made the radios and the television sets. The younger customers think it's the people who made the cars (Packards) or the telephone or Hewlett-Packard." The company officials readily admit that the name alone is not the sole reason for such success. The company provides quality products and bundles software, such as Microsoft Works, with its machines. Still the name has contributed by providing important differentiation for a "me-too" manufacturer.

In 1984 Hills Brothers Coffee bought out General Coffee Company, which was located in Miami. Hills Brothers needed the additional plant capacity. As part of the acquisition, Hills Brothers got the Chase & Sanborn trademark. Although the name had its heyday in the 1930s, Hills Brothers discovered that almost 90% of the people surveyed still recalled the trademark fondly from the days when Charley McCarthy pitched the product on the radio. The decision to revitalize the old name was explained by the company as being much easier than introducing a new name from zero. While the reintroduction of Chase & Sanborn will not drive Maxwell House or Folgers into the gutter, it still commands approximately 3% of the $4 billion coffee business and was accomplished with very little advertising support.

The power to differentiate isn't used only by small companies. Having been accused of churning out interchangeable boxlike cars in all of its divisions, General Motors is also looking for unique product differentiation. General Motors is estimated to own 360 trademark registrations. One of the names is LaSalle. In the 1920s and 1930s, the LaSalle was an elegant though somewhat less expensive automobile for people who didn't want to shell out for a Cadillac. The name is potentially going to be used for a new luxury car that is soon to be introduced by Cadillac. The Buick division of General Motors is planning to introduce a new four-door touring car in 1991. To give the car a cachet, it is likely to be named Roadmaster, a name that adorned a smooth-riding land yacht produced by Buick in the 1940s and 1950s.

General Electric purchased RCA Corporation in 1986. It recently decided to use the RCA name for a line of new microwaves, stoves, dishwashers, refrigerators, washing machines, and dryers. The company used the name because it wanted an instant reputation for quality. It doesn't seem to matter that the reputation had been built around a completely different business. Victor Alcott, manager of Industrial Design for GE appliances, told *Forbes* that "it takes far to much money to build a trademark with the inherent awareness of a well established name like RCA."

The extraordinary amount of dollars that are needed to introduce a new trademark makes the use of an established name, even if it had previously been discontinued for awhile, a much easier route. Extensive savings result from the instant recognition that already exists for an established name.

Another example of product differentiation through trademarking expanded the business of Sugar Foods Inc. Trademarks helped the company break out of the commodity business that had been its mainstay for more then 30 years. The company specializes in providing individual portion containers of condiments to the food service industry. Historically, Sweet 'N Low made up the bulk of the company sales. The company combined ingredients, packaged the mixture, and distributed it to the service companies. It was a nice business but had no where to grow.

For growth the company decided to focus on its expertise as a specialist in the packaging and distribution of individual portions of condiments. Other condiments that the company could exploit included lemon juice, mustard, relish, mayonnaise, and salad dressing. As a small company, however, an advertising and promotion campaign in the hundreds of millions of dollars was an impossible dream. But to get away from being a commodity packer, the company needed to use trademarks as a means to achieve differentiation. Sugar Foods approached manufacturers such as Sunkist, Vlasic, French's, and Tobasco and made arrangements to license their trademarks.

A typical contract with a trademark owner was established to run 10 years with options for renewal. No up-front fee was paid. Sugar Foods pays for the products it uses, plus royalty fees that run between 3% and 5% of gross dollars. The manufacturers derive a special benefit from the exposure of having thousands of tiny packets at food service outlets display their trademark. In 1986 Sugar Foods had sales of approximately $16 million. It expects $150 million in sales in the very near future. Once trademarks were introduced the company was able to grow.

**International Power**

In the United States it is reported that the average American is familiar with an unbelievable 1812 trade names. Trademarks also have international power. Consumers in the Soviet Union may not have much disposal income but they know exactly what they want. Listed below are five names that they know best:

1. Sony
2. Adidas
3. Ford
4. Toyota
5. Mercedes Benz

In Hungary and Poland the same names are on the list of best recognized trademarks.

All throughout Europe the trademarks we love in the United States are also the favorites of the British, French, German, and Italians. As Europe approaches the 1992 unification of economic markets, companies are acquiring other companies that possess trademarks which have already permeated the borders.

## Trademarks Are Becoming Scarce

Anyone that creates a new product has a problem. Odds are that the name that might be best for use with the new product is already taken, registered, and unavailable for use. Frank Delano, head of the product-naming firm of Delano, Goldman and Young Incorporated, says "any word or name a company thinks of three-quarters of the time is unavailable because someone else has claimed it already. Its becoming more difficult to find a name."

Between 1986 and 1988 the patent and trademark office received 130,000 trademark applications in the top ten categories. This included 21,000 for trademarks associated with publications, about 17,000 for advertising and business service companies, 16,000 for clothing, another 16,000 for miscellaneous services such as hotels, restaurants, and hospitals, 14,000 for food, 12,000 for scientific products, 10,000 for games and sporting goods, 10,000 for electrical apparatus, 9000 for educational entertainment companies, and 9000 for names of cutlery, machinery, and tools.

Anyone wishing to introduce a new product may have a very difficult time selecting a name that isn't already taken. The main problem is that the number of available trademarks that are appealing keeps shrinking. It becomes a challenge to find a name that does not have a conflict.

Anyone wanting to name a new car might look at some of the past successes involving the names of wild and speedy animals. They included Mustang, Cougar, Sting Ray, Pinto, and Firebird. What's left to use. Armadillo? Probably not.

In the United States the difficulty of coming up with an appealing trademark may ease a bit in the near future. The trademark law recently passed by Congress allows a company to register its trademark for 10 years compared with 20 years previously. To renew its registration of the trademark, the company has to prove it is using the name and not just holding it in reserve. But the best names are being used and as with anything else, scarcity makes trademarks more valuable. In the United States these days well established trademarks that are attractive to the consuming public are becoming scarcer. Old names with established recognizability are therefore being used on new products. Few names can be created that are not already owned by others. Investing in companies that already have established trademarks, while not actually being able to guarantee success, brings investors much closer to high rates of return.

---

Key Investment Concept #18

Investing in companies with a portfolio of trademarks is like an investment in rare and precious art.

---

## Let's Not Get Carried Away with Fads

Investment in powerful trademarks should not be confused with investment in fad names. A great deal of attention is given to merchandising products that have characters and names such as Bart Simpson, Teenage Mutant Ninja Turtles, Mario Brothers, and a host of other characters and names that are not likely to last in popularity for another year, let alone a decade. While quick profits are available from the exploitation of television and comic strip characters, there is a great deal of investment risk in assuming that sustained profits are possible.

When making an investment based on trademarks it is very important to identify and segregate trademarks that have significant longevity from those that are fads.

In the 1970s a hot design label carried the name Diane Von Furstenberg. A recent attempt by Donnkenny, Incorporated to revitalize the name completely failed. A spokesman for Lord & Taylor said "It wasn't seen as an innovative style anymore."

Some of the other "designer" trademarks that once had cachet are Sasson, Gloria Vanderbilt, and Halston. The marketing whizzes are trying to revive these trademarks. Gitano Group, Incorporated just purchased the dormant Gloria Vanderbilt trademark from Murjani Worldwide. The president of Gitano stated that "it would take millions of dollars to create a great designer name on our own."

Store buyers tend to be careful about products with which they fill their stores. Not only is the space limited but an established trademark is much more likely to get a buyer's attention. Bringing past trademarks "back from the dead," however, can be risky. Styles must be updated to conform with the latest trend and a new image must also typically be formed. Fifteen years ago Sasson was marketed as a saucy garment that was paraded by French bombshells at skin tight volumes. Today the products are being redesigned for the aging baby boomers aspiring for roominess in the cut of the products. Advertising has changed and is now aimed at a wholesome and family oriented image.

It is also nearly impossible to bring an old trademark back once it has been discounted. Experience at the retail level shows that once an upscale product and trademark are associated with lower priced goods recapturing the glitzy image of the past, along with premium price, is nearly impossible. Halston just ended a 6 year association with retailer J. C. Penney and Company. Its attempts to become reintroduced at uptown retailers has met with great frustration, leaving the company to pursue a new strategy—the mail order Halston couture collection. Most likely it will be impossible to recapture the attention of many upscale stores since its association with Penney's.

When investors consider the stock of a company that possesses trademarks, it must be remembered that just any old trademark won't do. Fads and "back-from-the-dead" can be just as risky as embryonic technological innovations.

## Even Trademarks Have Limits

When considering an investment in trademarks, the reputation of the industry is extremely important. It is difficult for a single trademark to overcome industry image problems. A poll conducted by

Peter D. Hart Research Associates asked consumers to identify industries, from a list of 22, in which consumers had the most and least amount of confidence. Winners included drugs, food, and foreign car makers. Industries in which consumers had the least amount of confidence included insurance, oil companies, and stockbrokers.

Experts also attribute poor image characteristics to combative advertising campaigns, which are popular in many industries. An example is the comparative advertising that continually dulls the television sets across America. McDonald's, Burger King, and Wendy's deride each other endlessly. The survey showed that fast food chains drew a strong negative response from almost one in five consumers.

Consumers that were surveyed about the companies or the industries in which they had the least amount of confidence picked airlines 43% of the time.

If investors are looking to place funds in companies with well recognized trademarks, they should consider that no amount of advertising can overcome a poor industry image.

Listed below are the best known and most highly regarded trademarks in the world according to a survey of 3000 consumers. Only one of the industries in which these names are used had a poor showing in the confidence survey. The combination of industry confidence and well-known trademarks represent a solid foundation for investment:

| | | | |
|---|---|---|---|
| 1. | Coca-Cola | 11. | Volkswagen |
| 2. | IBM | 12. | Mercedes |
| 3. | Sony | 13. | Pepsi-Cola |
| 4. | Porsche | 14. | Kleenex |
| 5. | McDonald's | 15. | Nestlé |
| 6. | Disney | 16. | Rolex |
| 7. | Honda | 17. | Jaguar |
| 8. | Toyota | 18. | Xerox |
| 9. | Seiko | 19. | Lipton |
| 10. | BMW | 20. | Hilton |

## Trademark Loyalty

Life-style surveys continue to tell researchers that the average shopper is pragmatic and professional but also under severe time constraint. Also, because of the time constraints, consumers are very often frustrated by product failures and corporate negligence in the area of customer service. On the rare occasion that customers find products that are satisfying, they tend to remain loyal. At the same time, the consuming public is pragmatic and will switch to equivalent products for the promise of savings if the switch can easily be accomplished. When in doubt, however, consumers tend to go toward established trademarks that they trust. As such, powerful trademarks are stronger than ever. Time constraints tend to dissuade consumers from trying something new that might fail.

*The Wall Street Journal* commissioned a survey recently entitled *American Way of Buying.* Two thousand consumers were surveyed by Peter D. Hart Research Associates. The survey presented 25 categories of products to the survey group. Presented in Exhibit 5-3 is a table that shows the 25 product categories and the percentage of users that are loyal to one trademark.

It is interesting to see that the trademark categories which topped 60% loyalty were cigarettes, mayonnaise, and toothpaste. For products such as garbage bags, athletic shoes, batteries, and canned vegetables, fewer than 30% of the surveyed consumers usually buy the same trademark.

Some of the characteristics that contribute to trademark loyalty are distinctive tastes, such as that found in certain cigarettes, and the image portrayed by the trademark such as the macho characteristics associated with Marlboro. The survey showed that loyalty tends to be stronger among older consumers. Higher wage earners also tend to be more trademark loyal. Some people speculate that wealthier consumers are busy and have less time to research products. Thus they tend to buy the highest quality as portrayed by trademarks with less emphasis on the type of savings presented by discount coupons. An established trademark can be seen as insurance that an acceptable amount of quality is associated with the trademark.

When considering a trademark investment, particular attention

*Exhibit 5-3*    Percentage of Loyal Customers

| Product Category | Percentage of Loyal Customers |
| --- | --- |
| Cigarettes | 71% |
| Mayonnaise | 65% |
| Toothpaste | 61% |
| Coffee | 58% |
| Headache remedy | 56% |
| Film | 56% |
| Bath soap | 53% |
| Ketchup | 51% |
| Laundry detergent | 48% |
| Beer | 48% |
| Automobile | 47% |
| Perfume/after-shave | 46% |
| Pet food | 45% |
| Shampoo | 44% |
| Soft drinks | 44% |
| Tuna fish | 44% |
| Gasoline | 39% |
| Underwear | 36% |
| Television | 35% |
| Tires | 33% |
| Blue jeans | 33% |
| Batteries | 29% |
| Athletic shoes | 27% |
| Canned vegetables | 25% |
| Garbage bags | 23% |

should be given to the type of product associated with the trademark. Investments in trademarks associated with the products at the high end of the loyalty list are stronger investments, are less likely to be affected by discounting and promotion programs, and probably will provide more stability in future earnings. At the low end of trademark loyalty, competitive actions and discount coupons and other promotions can shake the earnings stability of the company. In a sense, trademark power is dependent on product categories and the sometimes fickle nature of the consuming public.

When considering a trademark stock investment three key areas to study are: (1) the recognizability of the trademark, (2) consumer confidence related toward the industry, and (3) product loyalty.

## Trademark Leverage

When considering an investment, the focus should be on companies that have great trademarks and are constantly trying to make better use of those names. Examples of trademarks that have been extended successfully include Sunkist Orange Soda, Minolta Copiers, Levi Shirts, Levi Shoes, Del Monte Mexican Food, Woolite Rug Shampoo, Easy-Off Window Cleaner, Gerber Insurance, and Vaseline Intensive Care Skin Lotion.

Ten years ago Bic sold pens in the United States that were disposable. In rethinking the company's strategy, Bic decided that the strength of the company was in manufacturing inexpensive and disposable *products,* not just pens. The quality of Bic pens translated to dependability being associated with the name Bic. The company has used the strength of its name to introduce shavers, lighters, a Bic roller pen, and other writing instruments that are inexpensive to manufacture and are disposable.

Transition to trademark extension is not always easy. Arm & Hammer antiperspirant, Certs gum, Lifesavers gum, Sara Lee Chicken and Noodles Au Gratin, and Listerol used well known names in new product categories. Without distinction, sometimes the application of a trademark to a commodity product in an industry that is already well dominated by other participants won't yield satisfactory results.

Neve Savage of Cadwell, Davis and Savage, an advertising agency, has put together a ten point "life signs" test to determine if trademark images can be extended. Listed below are those ten points to consider:

1.   Does the product have new or extended uses? Arm & Hammer baking soda extended its usefulness by promoting it as a freshener for refrigerators.

2.   Is the product a generic item that can be enhanced by branding? Frank Perdue put his name on chickens and Sunkist did the same with oranges.

3.   Is the product category underadvertised? An example of this can be seen in many personal products such as tampons. Until

International Platex came along with huge advertising budgets, the marketing of these personal products was insufficient. The opportunity of underadvertised categories allowed market share to be captured.

4. Is there a broader target market? Procter & Gamble reversed declining Ivory soap sales in 1971 by promoting it for adults instead of just for babies.

5. Can disadvantages be turned to advantages? J. M. Smucker is the company that manufactures jams and jellies but had a difficult name and turned it to an advantage with an advertising slogan: "With a name like Smucker, it has to be good."

6. Can you cut price and build volume and profit?

7. Can you market unused by-products with the trademark?

8. Can you sell the trademarked products in a more compelling way? Pampers was not a successful product when it was advertised as a convenience for mothers. When the focus of the advertising was changed to benefiting babies by keeping them happier and dryer, sales soared.

9. Is there a marketplace or social trend to exploit?

10. Can you expand distribution channels?

## More Leverage

The power of trademarks also helped to establish a completely new company when three SmithKline Beckman executives founded Menley and James Laboratories. The founders of the company purchased 32 consumer products from SmithKline Beckman for $52 million. The products have annual sales that reached approximately $30 million. Included in the purchase are over-the-counter drugs such as ARM, an allergy relief medicine, and HOLD, cough suppressant lozenges. Also included were Contac, a cold remedy medicine, Ecotrin aspirin, and personal care products such as Rose Milk skin lotion.

The company gains a significant advantage over many start-ups. Its products are supported by well established trademarks with many years of customer loyalty.

Menley and James operates leanly. Product manufacturing is contracted out to other drug companies. Warehousing and distribution are handled by a contracting distributor. The main activity of the company executives at Menley and James is to lead a renewed marketing push for the trademarked products. In fact, the way in which the company is operating, using contract manufacturing and warehousing, is probably the most expensive way to obtain these services. At the same time, however, this allows the company executives to focus their attention on the most important aspect of their business—aggressive advertising and promotion of established trademarks.

This is an example of a new start-up company that was born with $30 million of sales on the first day and expects to reach $100 million in three to five years. Only through the power of trademarks was this possible.

Polaroid has a new way of selling cameras but it has nothing to do with the Polaroid name. The plan the company is thinking about is to use the Minolta name. Polaroid agreed to let the Japanese company sell the Spectropro, Polaroid's most expensive consumer instant camera in the United States, as the Minolta Instantpro. This is a highly unusual move. Polaroid has long said that it has one of the best known trademarks. It is unusual then to let someone else put their name on a Polaroid product. While instant cameras have shown poor sales growth during the last decade, 35mm cameras such as those sold by Minolta have dominated. Polaroid is looking for more ways to get more cameras in the hands of photographers so that it can sell more film.

The move by Polaroid not only let the company benefit from the Minolta name but also introduced the benefit of other intangible assets. Polaroid will also be able to take advantage of Minolta's superior marketing force in specialty camera stores. In addition, Polaroid will benefit from the sale of film. The agreement with Minolta does not allow Minolta to sell instant film for the cameras.

## Chattem, Inc.: Building with Trademark Rejects

Chattem Inc. was founded on a history of selling patented medicines through salespeople that used horse and buggies to travel to backwoods general stores.

From such a history the company has built itself on selected trademark niches. It has taken dud trademarks from the likes of Gillette and SmithKline Beckman and made them into winners. It is not so much marketing genius but an appreciation for small trademarks. The company concentrates on products that are no longer wanted by major corporations. One of the products is Sun-In, a peroxide hair lightener acquired from Gillette in 1974. Initially, the product had $500,000 in annual sales, which pretty much made it nonexistent to the billion dollar Gillette Corporation. Chattem bought the trademark of the product and by 1982 increased sales to $4 million.

Another acquisition involved a mud pack facial cleanser named Mudd. The product was initially pitched to teenage girls with the slogan "Mudd zaps zits." After acquiring the product line, Chattem pitched the name to old women as better prospects and within 7 years increased sales from $90,000 to $3 million.

The strategy employed by the company is to find small markets that are ignored by the giant cosmetic and drug companies and introduce strong trademarks that dominate the little markets. In addition, the company focuses on small niches of industrial chemicals. The strategy has allowed the company to achieve excellent sales growth against larger and better financed rivals while still achieving extraordinary profit levels on a consistent basis.

A 10 year investment in the company stock provided investors with an annual average compound return of 14.8%: much better than the return from the S&P 400 or the Dow Jones Industrial Average.

## Fragile Trademarks

The following list is not what you might think:

| | |
|---|---|
| Escalator | Kerosene |
| Trampoline | Linoleum |
| Dry Ice | Brassiere |
| Shredded Wheat | Zipper |
| Mimeograph | Thermos |
| Yo-Yo | Cellophane |
| High Octane | |

The preceding names were once proud, well known powerful *trademarks*. Now they are just names. The owners failed to take precautions that would have helped these names to be maintained as proprietary property with long prosperous lives. Unfortunately, they have passed into the domain of generic names, no longer proprietary. While there is always a possibility that a valuable trademark could be lost to the public domain of generic names, it is currently rare. Most corporations are extremely vigilant in their protection of valuable trade names. Protection against the misuse of valuable trademarks is a growing trend.

Harley Davidson Inc. provided information to federal agents recently about unauthorized and illegal use of the company trademarks on products being sold at the Wisconsin State Fair. In response, several vendors had products seized. Not all corporations are going to such lengths but the trend is clear. The value of the trademark can transcend its use on company products. Other manufacturers also make money by using Harley Davidson logos on other products. It is estimated that each year approximately $70 million worth of products are sold bearing the Harley Davidson trademarks for which the company receives between 6% and 15% as a royalty.

Over the past several years Harley Davidson has successfully curtailed the activities of over 1000 people who were using the Harley Davidson trademarks on an unauthorized basis.

Protecting the Kleenex name is conducted in a different manner by Kimberly Clark Corporation and for slightly different reasons. Harley Davidson doesn't want others to use their asset without providing the company with compensation. The problem facing Kimberly Clark isn't so much unauthorized use as the use of the Kleenex name as a generic name for facial tissues. The company name doesn't necessarily lend itself easily to licensing but the name is still misused. In order to head off the transition from proprietary trademark to public domain and generic garbage, the legal department at Kimberly Clark watches closely for misuse of the name. When misuse is discovered, the company makes sure that the offenders are notified that Kleenex is a trademark not to be confused with any old facial tissue.

Without strong efforts by a corporation it is quite possible that a few highly regarded proprietary names could become generic. Quite often Xerox is misused to describe any office copy machine. The same problem applies when many people refer to any four-wheel drive vehicle as a Jeep. While the loss of a proprietary name to the domain of generic-land is a possibility, the strong procedures to countermand this trend currently followed by most corporations, indicate the extreme value attached to trademarks. It is unlikely that stock investments based on strong trademarks would be lost to generics. But trademarks are being weakened by other activities.

## Trademarks Are Under Attack

Marketers have contributed to the erosion of trademark loyalty. The increase in spending on short-term promotions, discount coupons, and other short-term earnings generators can tarnish the effects of image-building advertisements. In fact, the two types of ad spending can work in conflicting ways. One advertisement explains to consumers about the long heritage of quality, service, dependability, and even patriotism to be associated with a certain product. Almost simultaneously the customer may find a discount coupon that deeply cuts the price and also undercuts the image-building message.

The trend toward quick promotions has been fueled by a short-sighted focus that has plagued all company operations and strategies during the 1980s. The focus is on near-term earnings, which can temporarily be boosted by price cutting promotions. However, this type of activity confuses customers and can be counterproductive to maintaining the stature, image, and prestige of many trademarks. Some of the strongest trademarks have never allowed promotional price cutting or discounts. Cross Pens are never put on sale. Other prestigious trademark names that can rarely be found on sale include Rolex, Rolls Royce, Hermes, and Glenlivet.

Marketers have strayed from principles that have traditionally driven the creation of trademarks. V. O. Budd Hamilton (of Procter & Gamble) said that the industry "should worry about and be unhappy with the current marketing environment." He goes on to say further that "franchises are not built by cutting prices but rather by offering superior quality at a reasonable price and clearly communicating that value to consumers."

Hamilton traced the roots of marketing problems to the early 1970s when price controls were instituted and then lifted. He said manufacturers raised prices and profits as a buffer against the possibility of future price controls. When consumers rebelled against the continuation of rising prices, companies shifted marketing dollars to promotions that cut prices. Hamilton said: "But as the promotions stakes were bid up, marketers further increased prices to maintain margins, thus creating a vicious circle of promotion and price escalation."

The result of escalating prices that are then cut by promotional activities confuses the consuming public. Consumers are overwhelmed by the confusion between image advertising, which establishes and maintains trademarks, and promotional activities, which cut prices. Hamilton says that "the real challenge is to develop advertising that can break through the clutter."

When assessing the value and longevity of the power associated with a trademark, it is sometimes difficult to see the "cracks" in time. But one of the most important factors that can be considered when assessing the power of a trademark is how the name is extended and used. In the early 1900s with the advent of a new high-speed V8 engine, Cadillac grabbed hold of the leadership position in quality cars. It used the innovation to differentiate itself and take the lead in prestige and mystique: a lead that it held onto for almost 50 years. General Motors destroyed the trademark image when it started to produce different Cadillac models to match the various market segments. Many observers credit the introduction of the Cimmaron, a Chevy Cavalier with extra chrome, as the fatal blow to the Cadillac image. Other "startegies" at GM standardized products across all divisions. Quickly, a Cadillac looked like a Buick or a Chevrolet or

---

Key Investment Concept #19

While investors in companies with significant trademarks are not likely to be able to influence management, it is important that when the image of a trademark begins to become tarnished that serious considerations to be given to liquidating the investment and moving on to a corporation that cherishes and protects the position and image of its trademarks.

certain Oldsmobiles. While General Motors is now trying to recover the mystique that was destroyed, it may be too late. Many others have filled the void left by Cadillac. They include Mercedes Benz, BMW, Jaguar, and Lexus. It can easily happen and go unnoticed initially. But trademark names are extremely fragile. As previously discussed, once the Halston name was used in association with J. C. Penney, it could never regain the exclusive image that once allowed extraordinary garment pricing.

## Investment-Grade Characteristics

Trademarks have many characteristics that are associated with high quality investments:

1. They are in short supply.
2. They have international exposure.
3. They can be used to leverage a company into new business areas.
4. They serve as foundations for building new companies.
5. They act as barriers to competition.
6. They have almost unlimited lives.
7. They contribute toward stable sales and earnings.

Trademarks also contribute to investment performance.

## Trademarks Boost Stock Returns

Trademarks are created and maintained by advertising. Companies that spend the most money on advertising are either creating or maintaining trademarks. It follows that companies spending the most money have some of the best known names. The question is: *Do well known trademarks contribute to stock performance?* The answer is definitely *Yes*.

Each year *Advertising Age* compiles a list of the "100 Leading National Advertisers." To make the list in 1990 companies had to spend over $108 million in the prior year. Philip Morris took the number one spot by spending over $2.0 billion in advertising to support its portfolio of famous trademarks. In aggregate, the Top 100 spent $32.2 billion in 1989. This spending created and maintained well known trademarks. Happily, this spending translates to positive stock performance.

A regression analysis is presented in Exhibit 5-4. It shows the relationship between advertisement spending and investment rates of return. For each company in the Top 100, advertising expenses were calculated as a percentage of company sales. This spending level was then compared to the investment rate of return achieved from a 10 year investment in the company stock. Exhibit 5-4 shows that *higher amounts of advertising on trademarks yield higher investment returns.*

---

### Key Investment Concept #20

Companies that have well known trademarks show superior investment returns.

---

Over the last 10 years the companies in the Top 100 have remained relatively stable. Consistent advertising is fundamental to

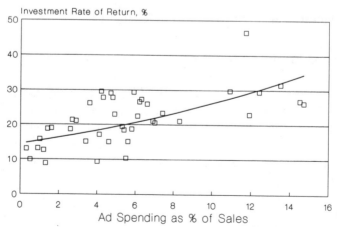

*Exhibit 5-4*  Advertising Spending Versus Investment Returns: Trademarks Enhance Stock Values

*Exhibit 5-5*  Consistent Advertisers

| Top Ten in 1980 | Top Ten in 1990 |
| --- | --- |
| Procter & Gamble | Philip Morris |
| General Foods | Procter & Gamble |
| Sears, Roebuck | General Motors |
| General Motors | Sears, Roebuck |
| Philip Morris | RJR Nabisco |
| K Mart | Grand Metropolitan |
| RJR Reynolds | Eastman Kodak |
| Warner-Lambert | McDonald's |
| AT&T | PepsiCo |
| Ford Motor | Kellogg |

nurturing and maintaining a trademark. As an example, Exhibit 5-5 shows that the Top Ten advertisers have changed little.

General Foods is still among the Top Ten as part of Philip Morris, which acquired the company in the mid-1980s. RJR Reynolds is also still in the Top Ten but it is currently a private company that is combined with Nabisco trademarks. Many companies have combined operations during the merger boom but the Top 100 advertisers are still mostly comprised of the same club members with the same valuable names, regardless of ownership. Analysis of the stock performance of the companies that own famous trademarks reflects the contribution to investment performance made by trademarks.

The analysis could not include all of the Top 100. Over half of the big spenders had to be eliminated. The U.S. government placed 36th on the list by spending $295 million on advertising but clearly doesn't possess stock performance measures suitable for inclusion in the study. Also eliminated were private companies, such as Hallmark Cards and Mars candy, for which stock performance measures were unavailable.

In general, companies were omitted from the study for the following reasons:

1. Stock values were unavailable for the entire 10 year period. Some were not public companies for the entire period and others are currently private companies.

| Company | Ad Spending as a % of Revenues | Return on Investment |
|---|---|---|
| Mobil | 0.3% | 13.0% |
| IBM | 0.5% | 9.9% |
| Ford Motor | 0.7% | 26.0% |
| Dow Chemical | 0.9% | 13.1% |
| American Express | 1.0% | 15.7% |
| General Motors | 1.2% | 12.6% |
| Goodyear | 1.2% | 8.8% |
| American Brands | 1.4% | 18.7% |
| Chrysler | 1.6% | 18.9% |
| Seagram | 2.6% | 18.6% |
| CPC Intl | 2.6% | 21.3% |
| Whitman | 2.9% | 21.0% |
| Marriott | 3.4% | 15.1% |
| Campbell Soup | 3.6% | 26.1% |
| Eastman Kodak | 4.0% | 9.3% |
| Pfizer | 4.1% | 17.1% |
| Gillette | 4.2% | 29.5% |
| Coca-Cola | 4.3% | 27.7% |
| MCA | 4.6% | 15.0% |
| Philip Morris | 4.6% | 29.0% |
| PepsiCo | 4.7% | 27.7% |
| Bristol-Myers Squibb | 4.7% | 22.9% |
| American Cyanamid | 5.3% | 19.4% |
| Time Warner | 5.4% | 18.4% |
| Tandy | 5.5% | 10.3% |
| SmithKline Beckman | 5.6% | 15.1% |
| American Home Products | 5.8% | 18.7% |
| H.J. Heinz | 5.9% | 29.3% |
| Colgate-Palmolive | 6.1% | 22.4% |
| Anheuser-Busch | 6.2% | 26.5% |
| Ralston Purina | 6.3% | 27.2% |
| Walt Disney | 6.6% | 25.9% |
| Johnson & Johnson | 6.9% | 21.0% |
| Procter & Gamble | 7.0% | 20.5% |
| Quaker Oats | 7.4% | 23.3% |
| Schering-Plough | 8.3% | 21.0% |
| Clorox | 10.9% | 29.7% |
| Hasbro | 11.7% | 46.5% |
| McDonald's | 11.9% | 22.9% |
| Hershey Foods | 12.4% | 29.4% |
| Wrigley | 13.5% | 31.5% |
| Warner-Lambert | 14.5% | 26.8% |
| Kellogg | 14.7% | 26.2% |
| S&P 400 | .................................... | 11.8% |
| DJIA 30 | .................................... | 12.0% |

*Exhibit 5-6*    Trademark Spending Yields High Stock Returns

2. Institutional spenders such as the U.S. government and the American Dairy Farmers Association do not possess value performance indicators.

3. The stock performance measures of telephone companies and airlines were considered to be more directly determined by the economic contributions of intangible assets beyond that of trademarks that are based upon regulation and exclusive business territories.

4. Department store corporations primarily advertise the trademarks of other companies and were not considered to represent direct links between trademark spending and stock performance.

The trend presented in Exhibit 5-4 clearly indicates that trademarks are associated with stock appreciation. The companies that comprise the trend data are listed in Exhibit 5-6.

Over the same 10 year period, the S&P 400 index showed a compound rate of return of 11.8%. A 10 year investment in the Dow Jones Industrial Average of 30 stocks would have provided a compound return of 12.0%. Of the 43 companies that were ultimately included in the study, all but three showed significantly better stock appreciation. The 40 winners have famous trademarks, all of which powerfully contributed to superior stock returns.

# 6

# PATENTS PROTECT
# CORPORATIONS . . .
# FOR AWHILE

An opportunity to enjoy monopolistic profits is granted to corporations with the issuance of a patent. During the 17 year life of the patent, its owner can exclude others from making, using, or selling the invention. During a large portion of this time, markets can be dominated and profit levels can be maintained at superior levels. Empires have been built on patents. Companies like Polaroid, Merck, and Xerox were founded on patents.

This would seem contrary to a society that is based on free competition but ultimately the patent system encourages technological development. Patents are a reward for those willing to spend huge amounts on research and development. Patents cover inventions, products, processes, designs, plants, and just recently animals. The cost of new inventions can be staggering.

During 1989, for example, member companies of the Pharmaceutical Manufacturers Association spent $7.3 billion in research and development. This represents an astonishing 16% of the total 1989 sales of $46.2 billion. It takes almost 3 years to get FDA approval for new drugs and sometimes much more. This doesn't include the time required to initially develop the drug. It is unlikely that such huge amounts of money and effort would be spent if competitors were allowed to instantly sell the same new drug. So, to encourage new inventions, Congress adopted the patent system as long ago as the Constitutional Convention.

## A Legal Monopoly

On September 5, 1787 the Committee on Detail reported to the [Constitutional] Convention that Congress should have the power:

"To promote the progress of science and useful arts, by securing for limited times to authors and inventors the exclusive right to their respective writings and discoveries."

That recommendation was unanimously adopted . . . without recorded debate, and the provision was incorporated into the final draft of the Constitution.[1]

"That Constitutional clause is highly unusual in that it instructs the Congress how to promote the progress of the useful arts—namely, by securing to inventors the exclusive rights to their discoveries. It is even more unusual in that nowhere else in the Constitution is there any provision for an exclusive right to be granted to any individual or group of individuals; only authors and inventors are so blessed. [2]

The enhanced value to a corporation from its patents is directly tied to the rights that are secured by our Constitution. Subject matter that can be patented is very broad as spelled out in the Constitution, including "any new and useful process, machine, manufacture, or

---

[1] *Journal of the Patent and Trademark Office Society,* "An Unanticipated,Nonobvious, Enabling Portion of the Constitution: The Patent Provision—The Best Mode," by Donald W.Banner, November 1987.
[2] See footnote 1.

composition of matter, or any new and useful improvement thereof." United States patents cover such innovations as genetically engineered organisms and methods for medical treatment such as surgical methods and blood diagnostics. The protected technology allows any associated enhancements of cash flow to be exclusively enjoyed over the remaining period of the patent life. The potential to enjoy exclusive profits for 17 years is substantial indeed. Patents would have questionable value if the covered innovation were open to common exploitation. The very existence of new inventions is questionable without a patent system. What individual would spend time to research if the efforts would not yield a personal benefit. And what investor would provide the necessary capital for development and commercialization if anyone else could later come along and take the product.

> Edwin Land, inventor and founder of Polaroid, said, "I must emphasize that the kind of company I believe in cannot come into being and cannot continue its existence except with the full support of the patent system." He later said, "The only thing that keeps us alive is our brilliance. The only way to protect our brilliance is our patents." [3]

Many important inventions were first discovered and developed by the small companies and by inventors with desire. Without the patent system, we would likely not have the economic power that we enjoy nor the quality of life we cherish.

The Continental Congress had in mind the creation of a country and system of self-government like none ever tried before: a system that protected the rights of individuals above all else; a system where the governing body had only the powers granted to it by its citizens. The protection of the fruits of inventive energies seems a natural extension of "The Miracle at Philadelphia."

Economic prosperity and military strength were imperative for the new experiment to work. By stimulating and encouraging innovation, the United States has achieved economic prosperity that all other systems of government can only envy.

---

[3] See footnote 1.

Probably the first international recognition of the eminence of American invention came at the Crystal Palace Exhibition in London in 1851. *The London Times* said, "It is beyond all denial that every practical success of the season belongs to the Americans." . . . And about the turn of the century, a Japanese official, Korekiyo Takahashi, was sent to the United States; he subsequently reported "We have looked about to see what nations are the greatest, so that we can be like them. We asked ourselves 'What is it that makes the United States such a great nation?' and we investigated and found that it was patents, and we will have patents." [4]

In 1790, three patents were granted. The first was issued to Samuel Hopkins and covered "A Process of Making Pot Ash and Pearl Ash." The following 60 years showed an average of under 500 inventions patented each year. Starting in the late 1850s, the innovative energies of the country began to accelerate with 1754 patents issued in 1854. Exhibit 6-1 shows the number of patent applications and issuances on inventions each year since 1790. The numbers exclude designs and botanical plants.

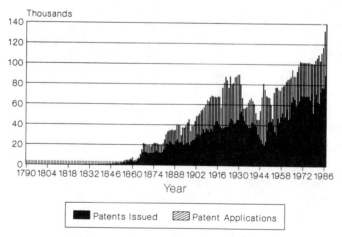

*Exhibit 6-1*    Patented Inventions 1790–1987

---

[4] See footnote 1.

Except for the depression of the 1930s and World War II, the number of patents issued each year has steadily increased. There are currently about 4.7 million patents covering a wide variety of inventions, designs, and botanical plants. Most recently, a patent was granted on a life form: a mouse that is genetically bred to develop cancer for use in medical research.

The number of patent applications on inventions hit a peak in 1930 at 89,554. The Great Depression was just beginning and emphasis on innovation was beginning to slow; survival took precedence over innovation. Also during the late 1930s Germany was the world leader in chemical technology but was not filing for patents in the United States. The overall trend continued to deteriorate until 1943. In 1943 a low point in patent applications was reached with only 45,493 applications. At this point World War II began to show signs of favorable resolution and attention once again returned to the future. Technology that was developed during the war was seen as having commercial viability. As a result, patent applications surged. The issuance of patents reflects these trends with a slight lag representing the period of time that was, and still is, needed for Patent Office review and action.

## Patent Rights Have Been Strengthened

Congress wanted to encourage innovation and disclosure but for many years the legal system denied inventors and companies the exclusivity granted in the Constitution.

During the period between 1948 and 1952, applications again dropped. This reflected a prevailing attitude that infringement suits were being used to hamper competition. An anti-patent reputation became associated with some of the federal district courts. Trying to uphold a patent in court was often a losing proposition. The benefits of having a patent were severely undermined. Infringers were relatively free to use the patented inventions of others with impunity. Innovation may not have been halted but disclosure was not being encouraged as originally intended by the Constitution. The struggle between patent laws and antitrust laws began to favor the elimination of all forms of monopoly, which included diminishing the rights of patent owners.

Little changed until 1980, when Congress recognized that a stronger patent system could help protect the U.S. economy and inventors from the growing influx of foreign competition. Stronger laws were passed and the budget for the U.S. Patent Office more than tripled to $300 million during the 1980s. Most important of all, the scales were tipped in favor of patent holders in 1982 when Congress established the Court of Appeals for the Federal Circuit (CAFC).

## Court of Appeals for the Federal Circuit

The Court of Appeals for the Federal Circuit is the only court that handles patent appeals throughout the nation. Its decisions have clarified and made uniform U.S. patent law. The rights of patent holders are more sacred than ever before. The values of valid patents reflect this new pro-patent legal climate and so do the values of the companies that own these patents.

Strengthening the patent system provides corporations with two major benefits, both of which can enhance the value of a company. The first obvious benefit is relief from the economic damage that is inflicted by infringers. Second, another source of revenues from licensing becomes viable. Later in the book, licensing is presented as a powerful strategy for exploiting technological property and as a new source of revenues. The prevailing pro-patent attitude supports this economic windfall.

## Preliminary Injunction Stops Infringers Cold

Under 35 USC P 283 (1952)

> courts may grant injunctions in accordance with the principles of equity to prevent the violation of any right secured by patent, on such terms as the court deems reasonable.

Previous to 1982, when infringement cases were initiated, preliminary injunctions were granted only when there was a "reasonable likelihood" that the infringed patent could be proved to be valid and infringed. While preliminary injunctions were typically granted in trademark and copyright cases, they were seldom granted for patents. The owner of the infringed patent was required to prove the validity of the patent in order to be granted a preliminary injunction. Only where prior court decisions had found the patent valid was this really possible. Otherwise, validity could not be proved until the case was tried. Meanwhile, infringers were free to continue violating the rights of patent owners. Infringing on an existing patent was not a very risky decision because an infringer could continue to exploit an infringed product or service while court cases dragged out. CAFC decisions turned the tables in favor of patent holders.

Preliminary injunctions are more readily granted. Infringers quickly find that their multi-million dollar manufacturing facilities can be shut down as they are driven out of the infringing business.

### Presumed Validity Puts Infringers on the Defensive

Currently, the CAFC standard has placed the burden of proving a patent invalid upon the infringer. Infringers must provide clear and substantial proof of invalidity. Otherwise, the patent owner is considered to have a valid patent.

This attitude, of presumed validity, is very powerful and makes infringement very costly and risky. Substantial investments by infringers can be rendered worthless. Infringement is more costly than ever and this new attitude by CAFC strengthens our patent system, making patents more valuable than ever before.

### Damage Awards in the High-Tech Battleground

Another shift enhancing patent values is the willingness of juries to grant huge awards. In addition, where willful infringement is proved, the damage award can be increased to three times the actual amount of damages. Companies that possess intellectual property see litigation as a competitive weapon and a means to assure that they are able to exploit these properties to the fullest potential in an increasingly competitive environment. Today there is a very aggressive use of patent rights. In some cases, suits are filed as a new source of revenue. The cost of infringement can be staggering.

- The case of *Smith International, Inc.* v. *Hughes Tool Company* is illustrative of this point. A damage award to Hughes of

$205.4 million regarding a patent infringement case was the cause of Smith's bankruptcy filing in 1986.

○ Eastman Kodak was driven from the instant photography market, having been found to have infringed on Polaroid patents. Kodak was forced to close its operations and was ordered to pay $1 billion to Polaroid as compensation for damages. This represents almost 7 times the 1989 net income for Polaroid of $145 million.

○ Mattel Inc. was found to have infringed on the flexible track invention of Jerome H. Lemelson in marketing its Hot Wheels line of miniature race cars. Mattel has sold over $700 million of the cars and track since their introduction 21 years ago. Mr. Lemelson was awarded $71 million.

○ Procter & Gamble collected $125 million from two companies that infringed on patents covering cookies that are crisp on the outside and chewy on the inside.

○ Monoclonal Antibodies, a biotechnology company, was forced to stop selling products that accounted for 80% of its revenues after losing an infringement battle. It was almost forced out of business.

The risk of infringement is being taken beyond the corporate level. The May 1988 issue of *Intellectual Property Happenings* reports that a recent case involving a software lawsuit alleging copyright infringement and unfair competition resulted in a $1.6 million verdict against the president of the defending company.

Clearly, the high risks of infringement will deter such actions in the future. The value of intellectual property is correspondingly enhanced.

Just a few of the other major companies that are involved in infringement lawsuits are:

IBM
Intel
NEC
Apple Computer
Genentech

Eli Lilly
Medtronics
Lotus Development
Samsung
Advanced Micro Devices
Microsoft Corporation
Ashton-Tate Corporation
Hewlett-Packard Company
Ford Motor Company
Ninetendo of America, Inc.

Favorable infringement decisions carry significant economic benefits for companies. Competitors are forced to abandon markets. The winners are then free to enjoy whatever level of premium pricing that the market will tolerate. A larger market share means higher levels of volume, which allow implementation of manufacturing efficiencies as previously discussed. Licensing becomes a viable source of additional revenues. All of these translate to strong profit margins and higher stock prices.

Damage awards are supporting the rights of patent holders and the value of the companies that own them. More than ever the legal system in the United States is working to protect and enhance the value of intellectual property. Stock values will directly reflect this trend.

---

Key Investment Concept #21

Infringement lawsuits can be very profitable investments.

---

Purchasing the stock of a company that has filed an infringement lawsuit can potentially provide a windfall. The benefit to shareholders can be direct, as in the case of Polaroid where shareholders have already been promised that they will directly receive a portion of the damage awards as a special dividend. Indirect benefits are also possible, occurring when the damage award is used by the company to reduce debt, finance new ventures, or complete acquisitions. If the stock is fundamentally sound, a potentially large damage award is a bonus and may be worth making part of an investment portfolio.

Patience is vital. Court cases can drag out for years while the company spends millions of dollars for legal advice. Jerome Lemelson started his lawsuit with Mattel in 1977 and Polaroid has been battling with Kodak for more than a decade.

## Champerty Investments

An even more direct investment in infringement lawsuits is possible through a *champerty* investment. Champerty investments involve unrelated investors who fund litigation for a share of the future damage awards.

A group of investors contributed $4 million in 1981 to fund a legal battle against ComputerLand. ComputerLand lost, providing the investor group with a successful litigation and a payback of an estimated $63 million, representing a compound rate of return of 36%.

Participation in champerty investments is risky. The lawsuit could be lost and with the original funds having gone to cover legal costs, the partnership won't have any assets to liquidate. Another risk is the possibility of running out of funds during the litigation process. Without any guarantees for success, the investor group may need to contribute additional funds to carry on the battle and protect the original investment. There is also the risk of counterclaims against champerty litigation. In some states, investing in lawsuits is illegal. The laws aim to protect the legal system and society against the burden of frivolous and speculative lawsuits.

Champerty investments are well suited for wealthy investors that can accept the risk of total loss. Small investors, however, can participate through stock ownership in Refac Technology Development Corporation. Refac has been buying patent rights and suing companies that infringe or stopped making royalty payments. Most recently, the company made $2 million of profits from revenues of $12 million. The company trades over-the-counter. More details about this company are provided in Chapter 8.

## Antitrust Law Conflicts Have Vanished

Patents grant exclusivity and antitrust laws work to eliminate monopolies. For quite awhile these two were seen to be in conflict. Licensing limitations by patent owners and the acquisition of similar patents by a single company were seen as restrictive to a competitive economic environment. New thinking sees our intellectual property laws as a complement to the encouragement of a competitive environment.

The Justice Department is more likely than ever to see intellectual property rights as enhancements of competition. First, patent laws create an incentive for companies to research, develop, and commercialize new products and services, which can be delivered in a more efficient manner. In addition, the laws encourage the disclosure of information that would otherwise be jealously guarded. Through licensing, this information can be shared and exploited in the most efficient manner.

Royalties go hand in hand with value. The strength of patents and the risk associated with infringement allow patent owners to negotiate higher royalties.

International Business Machines has recently embarked on a campaign to vigorously enforce its patents and to raise patent license rates. In a recent article that appeared in *MIS Week,* July 4, 1988, David La Riviere, a former IBM patent attorney, attributed this new attitude in part to changes in the federal law. La Riviere was quoted as saying "Patent holders now have a 70 to 80 percent chance of having their patents enforced, compared with 20 percent five or six years ago, because of the change in attitude by the courts."

Legal enhancements to the value of intellectual property are not limited to technological assets.

The Senate has just passed the first major changes in the federal trademark law since 1946.[5]

---

[5] *Intellectual Property Happenings,* "Major Change in Trademark Law Coming Soon,"May 1988, p. 1.

If approved, the new law will permit a trademark application to be filed as long as there is intent to use the mark. Previously, an application could not be filed until the mark had actually been in commercial use. In addition, a proposed federal law has a provision covering anti-dilution.

> The new provisions protect famous registered marks from unauthorized uses which lessen their distinctiveness and therefore their commercial value. [6]

Recently Toys R Us was successful in its legal action in forcing a New York company to refrain in the use of the name Auto Parts R Us.

## Software Protection Is Still Evolving

Technological developments are moving faster than the law. Software hasn't fared as well as patented inventions. Software is covered by copyrights. Unlike a patent, copyright protection is more limited, covering only the expression of an idea and not the idea itself. Patents protect original, nonobvious, and useful ideas. Others are excluded from using the idea. Copyrights protect only the expression of an idea. The difficult issue in software protection is defining the difference between the program function and its expression. The function cannot be protected exclusively, just as a book about traveling to Europe cannot belong to only one author. The words of a book cannot be copied. The programming code for a software program can also be protected against unauthorized copying. The difficulty arises when a different programming code is used to develop a competing program, say, for word processing, that has the same "look and feel" as a protected program.

The manner in which a software program user interfaces with the program refers to its "look and feel." Apple's Macintosh computer uses a very friendly graphical screen display. The display includes pop-up menus, windows of information, and graphic characters. Current litigation centers around whether the "look and feel"

---

[6] See footnote 5.

aspect of software programs can be protected. The amounts involved are in the billions.

For now, the "look and feel" of business in the software industry is free-for-all litigation.

## When Protection Runs Out

At the end of the 17 year patent protection, enhanced profits can falter; corporate value can follow.

In the pharmaceutical industry, generic drugs hit the market as pioneering drugs lose patent protection. One study shows, however, that even after 5 years of competition the pioneering drug can still maintain 50% of its market share. Pricing levels have usually dropped significantly due to competition, but something is better than nothing.

When patents expire, the competition can move in. Market share can be eroded, competitive pricing drives down revenues, and earnings can fall for the company that is too dependent on the patented product. Falling common stock prices aren't far behind.

## All Is Not Lost When Patents Expire

After patents expire, all the economic advantages will not necessarily be lost. The period of exclusivity is an opportunity to establish other barriers to competition. When these barriers are properly established, the market dominance and profitability that were initially created by patented technology can be maintained. Economic benefits are still enjoyed from the company from other assets, some of which may be intangible, as the sources of profits and superior investment returns. Protection of these economic benefits is transferred to other competitive barriers. Important competitive barriers include:

Established trademarks
Large capital investments
Distribution channels
Economies of scale
Government regulation

Initially, a company can exclusively provide product characteristics that customers find desirable based on the patent. Market share dominance is controlled by the exclusivity that is conveyed by the patent. The trademark associated with the new product might initially be unimportant. Over time, however, customer loyalty can be transferred to a specific trademark. Customers can be taught through advertising to associate the desirable product characteristics more with the product trademark. By the time the patent expires, competitors may find that the ability to capture market share will be hindered by customer loyalties and perceptions. Penetration of this barrier will require significant advertising expenses, which can at least in the beginning cause new entrants into the market to sustain significant losses.

The head start that patents provide can allow the company to dominate the market. Large sales volumes provide significant opportunities to enjoy economies of scale in areas such as manufacturing, sales force utilization, and the negotiation of raw materials contracts. Manufacturing facilities can be built to optimize unit costs. New entrants into the market will be required to invest heavily in capital assets, which may be poor investments if sufficient market share is not captured. Until then, losses can mount.

Depending on the product, additional shelf space and distribution networks may not be available to accommodate another entrant into the market. During the protected period, a strong distribution network can be established. Duplicating this aspect of market penetration is another formidable barrier.

Government regulations can cause another delay in the introduction of me-too products. Pollution controls, licensing requirements, and agency approvals, such as FDA approvals for drugs, can delay competitors and add significantly to the cost of market entry.

Patents expire but economic contributions are not automatically lost. Exhibit 6.2 illustrates the transference of economic value from a declining patent value to other assets such as trademarks.

It may seem that patents are providing limitless exploitation of economic benefits. This, however, is far from true. Competitors still have another option in the form of advancing innovation. By creating new inventions of their own and patenting the advanced tech-

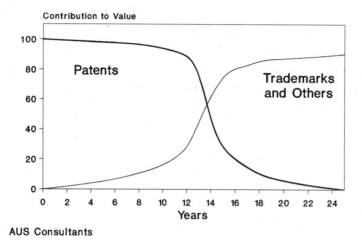

AUS Consultants

*Exhibit 6-2*   Protection Can Transfer to Other Intangible Assets

nology, the same technique that helped establish a formidable collection of competitive barriers can be used to penetrate the market. Just as Congress envisioned, patents help to advance the proliferation of innovation.

## Summary

Intellectual property is clearly a dominant factor that touches all our lives. It is becoming one of the most important assets among the collection of assets that are used by companies. Without intellectual property, a corporate investment becomes a collection of fixed assets manufacturing a commodity product in a competitive industry. Low profits usually come out of such mediocre investments. Stock prices have very little fuel for moving to higher levels.

The substantial value that intellectual property represents is getting more attention than ever before. Many companies no longer view licensing as a means by which to earn a few extra dollars. The attitude toward intellectual property licensing has shifted to a view whereby the full potential of intellectual property value can and must be realized. Just as idle floors of a corporate building are leased to others, intellectual property value is being exploited; idle assets are not to be tolerated in our increasingly competitive global environment. The focus has shifted and is more enlightened. Underutilization of intangible assets is not to be tolerated.

Beginning with the first sharpened stone, technological innovation has contributed to the enhancement of life and can now contribute more than ever before to rising stock prices.

# 7

# THE CARE AND FEEDING OF INTANGIBLES

Just as buildings and machinery require continued maintenance, intangible assets need care and nurturing. All the intangible assets that have been discussed are susceptible to deterioration from internal forces as well as external ones. Internal forces of deterioration are predominantly caused by neglect or misuse. External forces are the challenges brought on by competitors. This chapter discusses the ways in which intangible assets can deteriorate along with examples of what the best companies are doing to keep their intangible assets current and viable.

## Research Efforts Are Rewarded

The primary benefit derived from continually nurturing intangible assets is best exemplified by the technology of the pharmaceutical industry. An analysis of six pharmaceutical companies shows that continued research efforts are rewarded. The number of patents awarded to these companies when compared to the 10 year compounded rate of return earned by investors shows that superior investment returns are associated with the research efforts that yielded patents. Exhibit 7-1 shows the number of patents that were granted to six companies between 1979 and 1988. The total number of patents for the entire period is also presented along with the 10 year investment returns earned by holding the stock of these companies.

Warner-Lambert shows the highest rate of return at 24.4%. Second place goes to Merck, with the highest number of patents, but investors only achieved, a 23.9% return. Merck has received 1283 patents between 1979 and 1988 but investors in the stock earned slightly less. The slight advantage of Warner-Lambert may be attributed to the rapid pace at which the company obtained patents since 1984, when it obtained only 49 patents. By 1989 it had obtained 113.

Upjohn received 1178 patents during the period but only provided a 21.0% rate of return to investors. Of all the companies, Upjohn received the lowest number of patents in the most recent year, 1988. As the number of patents falls, the rate of return is lower. Generally, the relationship between recently obtained patents and investment returns prevails.

In general, investors have been keenly rewarded for holding on to these research intensive companies. All the companies exceeded the returns earned by the S&P 400 and the Dow Jones Industrial Average. Continued research pays off.

| Company | Total Patents 1979–1988 | Compound Investment Return | NUMBER OF PATENTS ISSUED PER YEAR | | | | | | | | | |
|---|---|---|---|---|---|---|---|---|---|---|---|---|
| | | | 1988 | 1987 | 1986 | 1985 | 1984 | 1983 | 1982 | 1981 | 1980 | 1979 |
| Warner–Lambert | 622 | 24.4% | 113 | 118 | 101 | 73 | 49 | 34 | 25 | 37 | 36 | 36 |
| Merck | 1283 | 23.9% | 125 | 123 | 103 | 105 | 135 | 114 | 135 | 160 | 156 | 127 |
| Upjohn | 1178 | 21.0% | 15 | 26 | 66 | 66 | 107 | 73 | 122 | 337 | 170 | 196 |
| Eli Lilly | 881 | 20.7% | 68 | 85 | 82 | 107 | 80 | 74 | 104 | 112 | 85 | 84 |
| American Home Products | 444 | 20.5% | 69 | 46 | 38 | 49 | 32 | 24 | 43 | 52 | 52 | 39 |
| Pfizer | 728 | 17.3% | 63 | 67 | 72 | 72 | 89 | 61 | 72 | 92 | 75 | 65 |

*Exhibit 7-1*    Drug Industry Patents and Investment Returns

## Research Programs: More Than Hit or Miss

A study conducted by the Office of the Chief Economist of the Security and Exchange Commission showed that company announcements indicating a plan to increase spending on research and development had a positive and immediate effect on the stock price of the companies that were studied.

---

Key Investment Concept #22

Research and development spending increases are positive for stock investments.

---

Investors should be especially wary of companies that announce plans for research and development spending reductions.

## Assessing Research and Development Quality

When assessing the results of research and development, measuring the number of patents produced or research papers written is only the first step in analyzing the benefits of R&D efforts. The most important measure of research and development success is an analysis of the number of new product introductions that are derived from research and development. 3M is well known for requiring each individual division to have a significant percentage of total sales derived from new product introductions.

The need for new product research is important because it is only through new products derived from innovative research that a company can sustain real growth. Otherwise, imitation products only embroil the company in fights for market share in mature industries.

In addition to new products, the other side of the research and development equation focuses on process research and not just new product research. Process research provides a company with new techniques to improve internal processes. Xerox is reorienting its R&D effort to focus on two areas. The first area provides improvements for ongoing products such as photocopiers. The other focuses on new fields that can provide new products. When considering and studying a company that is primarily comprised of technological know-how, the amount of money being spent on research and development is an important clue about the future prospects for the company. Further analysis, however, is required to understand the way in which research and development efforts are focused.

A review of the top 200 recipients of U.S. patents in 1989 included corporations, universities, and institutions from all over the world. United States based corporations accounted for over 50% of the patents achieved. The U.S. company that received the greatest amount of patents in 1989 was General Electric with 818. Following behind were IBM, Eastman Kodak, Westinghouse, DuPont, Dow Chemical, General Motors, Texas Instruments, Motorola, and AT&T. A correlation, however, of investment returns on a 10 year stock-holding with patents does not closely relate. Something else must be considered—quality of research.

Superior financial performance and investment results are associated with companies that produce quality patents from a disciplined research and development program. In *The New York Times,* March 7, 1990, an article entitled "Novel Technique Shows Japanese Out-pace Americans in Innovation" describes the technique that is being used by the federal government and other companies to assess the quality of newly issued patents. The method is based on the number of prior works that new patents cite in establishing novelty. This quality measurement methodology is based on the assumption that patents of high quality and importance are cited more often.

Application of the methodology is reported to show that, as early as 1976, patents awarded to Japanese inventors were cited more frequently than those awarded to Americans. A patent that is cited most often means that the innovative idea is widely recognized by other inventors. Some patents, arguably the most important, have been cited more than 100 times. A study conducted by Computer Horizons, a consulting company in Haddon Heights, New Jersey, indicates that some of the most highly cited patents are concentrated in the "hottest areas" such as semiconductor electronics, photography, photocopying, pharmaceuticals, pharmaceutical chemistry, and automotive technology.

## Continued Success from Focused Research Development

The goal of research is to bring new products to market faster and more often than the competition. Companies that hit the market first usually command premium prices and can capture a dominant amount of market share. Assessment of R&D programs is therefore one of the most important areas of fundamental analysis. Investors must look closely at the primary source of growth—new product development.

Successful research programs focus on three areas:

1. Improvement.
2. Evolution.
3. Innovation.

*Improvement* involves constant efforts to improve quality, to drive down manufacturing costs, and to incorporate features that are demanded by customers. The best known improvers had traditionally been the Japanese companies that copied successful American products and added reliable features. The improved products eventually surpassed the original items that were copied.

*Evolution* is described as the use of an established product, process, or service on which the next generation can be launched. An example is Sony. The company was based on the introduction of a small portable radio, which was later followed by the original Walk-Man which played cassette tapes as well as contained an AM-FM radio. Later, the product evolved further by allowing the consumer to portably enjoy compact discs. The product was further evolved with the recent introduction of a Watch-Man television set.

*Innovation* represents the next generation of technology. It involves basic research and the goal of incorporating new discoveries into useful products. Innovation is the core of growing companies but cannot serve alone as the source for continued growth and success.

All three of these research elements must be incorporated into the research and development effort. Otherwise, continued success by technological companies is not likely.

Listed below are company characteristics that denote the presence of a successful R&D program. Successful research programs Regularly:

1. Introduce new products to the market more often than competitors.
2. Introduce new products that possess meaningful technological advantages.
3. Introduce new products faster than competitors.

An article entitled "Turning R&D into Real Products" was featured in *Fortune*, July 2, 1990. In the article, the hope for American business is described as the process whereby innovative discoveries by scientists are turned into useful and lucrative new products. Historically, corporate research programs operated on an intuitive and "hit or miss" basis. The formula used by AT&T in research efforts was simple. "Hire brilliant scientists, turn them loose in search of basic knowledge, and wait for breakthroughs of vast commercial potential." The unfortunate consequence with this procedure was that American businesses proved to be very skillful at making basic discoveries but poor at transforming the discoveries into products. The environment within which research operations were performed didn't necessarily encourage capitalizing on the innovations.

The trend of American business is now to focus the attention of R&D programs into professionally managed organizations that combine exploratory encouragement with measurement techniques that count real product introductions. The trend can be characterized by the statement of Arno Penzias, the Nobel Prize winner at Bell Labs, when he said: "Five years ago managers at Bell Labs didn't even use the word customer. Now each of us has two jobs: working in corporate research and serving on a team connected to one of AT&T's product areas."

The trend in R&D facilities is to create an atmosphere where basic researchers work side by side with product experts. Gone are the isolated science laboratories where fabulous discoveries sat idly on work benches because product managers were unaware of their existence. A harmonious environment that fosters high-tech town squares allows business gossip to encourage application of innovations into new products.

## Casualties of Advancing Technology

There is little question that innovation can provide exciting improvements, but the lack of it can be disturbing. The external forces by competitors that advance technology has changed the success of many major corporations. Companies that were once in the Fortune 500 do not even exist today. One of the implications of innovation in our society is that one must keep up or perish.

Delivering telegrams was once an occupation for thousands of young men who scurried about on bicycles delivering the most important information of the day. Not only is Western Union a dramatically changed company but its no longer a big customer for bicycle manufacturers.

Mechanical calculators were once produced by the truckload at Friden. They were large, heavy, noisy, expensive, slow, prone to failure, extremely limited in capabilities, and required regular maintenance. Most engineers kept a slide rule close at hand for trigonometry and other such calculations. Today, the solution to mathematics is pocket sized, inexpensive, powerful, and disposable. So inexpensive are these Friden replacements that it is cheaper and simpler just to buy new ones if they ever fail. The reliability of these devices, however, usually means that we are more likely to lose the calculator before it is possible to break it. Companies like Texas Instrument, Casio, Sharp, and Hewlett-Packard were quick to see the future and either developed the new calculator technology or expanded on it.

Piston aircraft engines were the domain of Curtiss Wright. Their dominance in the field even allowed them at one time to begin a national network of airports. Their technology helped win World War II. Today, General Electric and Pratt & Whitney dominate the aircraft jet engine industry. Curtiss is subdividing and leasing the giant industrial complexes that once allowed America to fly.

Coal-fired locomotive train engines were manufactured by Baldwin American Locomotive Co. The company failed to recognize the potential of the diesel engine. It failed to keep up with technology and that cost the company its survival.

Vinyl records are fading into history. An article in *The New York Times*, April 1, 1990, entitled ''Recording Enters a New Era, and You Can't Find It on LP,'' clearly illustrates that advancing technology is unforgiving. The long-playing record album ''LP'' has been the medium for distributing music in the United States for decades, but advancing technology will soon make the LP a collectible. In 1989 LP record albums counted for only 4% of recording industry sales in the United States. David J. Steffen, senior vice president of Sales and Distribution at A&M Records, said: "There is an entire generation that has never owned a turntable." Technology that has surpassed the vinyl record takes the form of cassette tapes and compact discs. Many music stores have even stopped carrying vinyl records.

Investors that focus on technological companies must remember a vital rule: every new product, process, or service begins to become obsolete on the day that it is introduced. The initial profits and superior investment returns may quickly fade unless a thoughtfully managed research program becomes part of the corporate strategy.

## Some Trademarks Are Very Fragile

Care and feeding are more critical for some industries than for others. In some cases, image represents the majority of what is being purchased and once faded very little remains. An example of trademarks requiring continuous care can be found in the cosmetics industry. For the most part, cosmetics companies are basically selling hope. Hope that a blemish can be hidden, hope that eyes can be brightened, hope that wrinkles can be faded, hope for the appearance of health and the cloaking of age. As such, a great deal of money can be charged for a product that doesn't cost much to make. The cosmetics industry is characterized by the ability to mix materials that are worth pennies and sell the product for dollars. This type of environment provides extraordinary profits and attracts an extensive number of competitors. Hope and image are the most expensive ingredients and continuous care and feeding, as accomplished by expensive advertising, are the primary components in the cosmetics industry.

Some of the high prices of hope include:

$20 for lipsticks
$100 for a jar of skin cream
$50 for eye shadow

Maturing baby boomers and stabilized demographic trends have cut the fantastic growth rate that was experienced in the industry over the past decade. The problem of sluggish sales is further exacerbated by the higher costs to advertise. A story in *Forbes*, September 18, 1989, entitled "How Different Can a Seventeen Dollar Lipstick Be from a Three Dollar Version?" indicated that "American women are buying a smaller and smaller percentage of their cosmetics at department stores." This means big trouble for the upscale manufacturers such as Christian Dior, Chanel, and Este Lauder. Customers are shifting to the purchase of cosmetics products such as lipstick and moisturizers at supermarkets and drugstores. The pressures of career and family have eliminated the luxury of visiting downtown department stores. The mass marketers such as Maybelline and Neutrogena are capturing much of the market share from the upscale cosmetics companies.

Product parity and technological advances are putting extraordinary pressure on high priced hope. The low and medium priced product lines have been improved in recent years. Trading down from the upscale department stores is not much of a compromise anymore. A hypoallergenic ophthalmologist mascara from Maybelline runs for under $4 while the same product with the Yves Saint Laurent trademark costs about $20. In addition to technical parity, consumers are doubting the veracity of hyped trademarked skin creams, moisturizers, and anti-aging treatments. The consuming public is finally coming to believe that there are no miracles. Hope still drives buying activities but when the same technological parity can be purchased at almost 10% of the glitz name the high-priced products come under attack.

As economic downturns occur, some trademarks will prevail and possibly even prosper. During times of uncertainty consumers may tend to purchase products with which they feel most comfortable. A reliable "friend" from which no unhappy surprises are expected is the call of the time during economic uncertainty: especially if the "old friend" doesn't require bank loans to purchase.

Not all conspicuous consumption and upscale products are as fragile as cosmetics. Driving a BMW can make a statement about your purse and your taste. Sporting a Rolex watch, Gucci loafers, or Burberry raincoat makes similar statements. The problem with cosmetics is that no one knows whether you are made-up with a $3 lipstick or a $20 lipstick. Lipstick and eye shadow, once applied, do not announce to the world that the woman wearing them has arrived, unless the consumer carries the branded bottle around.

As an uncertain economic period approaches, certain trademarks like those of the upscale cosmetics will be extremely susceptible to market share erosion. The beneficiaries will be companies like Maybelline, a subsidiary of Shering Plough, Noxelle, which manufactures Cover Girl, and Neutrogena, which has speciality skin care offerings.

Trademarks indeed possess great powers. They can almost call customers over to the sales counter. Many have emotional appeal for loyal buyers. Yet, the trademark must be coupled with product or service characteristics that are desirable and sustained. Otherwise, the trademark approaches the condition of being a fad, which can have a rough time as economic growth slows.

## Advertising Budgets Are More than a Luxury

Ralston Purina was recently featured in a *Forbes,* August 21, 1989, article entitled "Chow Down". The company has built a successful collection of well known trademarks that include Dog Chow, Cat Chow, Hostess Twinkies, Eveready, and Wonder Bread. In 1988, the company apparently sacrificed advertising and promotion outlays in order to sustain level earnings. Sales of the pet food business are significantly down as a result. In 1988, advertising and promotion were increased at an amount that was less than the pace of inflation. In a competitive industry, the other players are not forgiving of mistakes and take every advantage. Competitors maintained and expanded higher advertising budgets. In response to eroding market share, Ralston had to step up its spending with advertising and promotion costs scheduled for 1990 to rise nearly 16%. However, as the company races to provide the care and feeding that were neglected, competitors continue to spend heavily.

The Eveready battery business, which was purchased from Union Carbide, is the number 2 battery seller behind Duracell. While Duracell, the number 1 battery seller, spent approximately $33 million on advertising in 1988, Ralston spent only $22.5. This low amount of spending is no quick way to move out of the number 2 position. It might also cause the loss of more market share to Duracell. In addition, the battle for market share intensified as Kodak entered the field with its own alkaline battery.

## Special Problems for Perrier

In 1990, Perrier was found to contain small amounts of benzene. Improper cleaning of bottling machines in France contaminated a production run, filling the United States with contaminated product. Not only was the sparkling water tainted but also the image of purity on which the company based its sales was in question. The company quickly pulled all of its product from the U.S. shelves and faced a critical problem during the period of time it took to restock the United States. The problem involved repairing and maintaining a well positioned image of purity without any product in the stores which could prove the point. This example goes beyond the typical problem of care and feeding but it clearly shows the vulnerability of even the best trademarks.

The company established an $8 million print and radio advertising effort to announce that "the problem has been fixed" and there "was never a health or safety problem". The ad campaign then went on to maintain top-of-the-mind awareness based on the theme "worth waiting for."

## Care and Feeding Take More than Money

Care and feeding also require continued attention to trends. A well regarded trademark can lose its luster if the consumer perceives that the product is not keeping pace with changes. White Shoulders is a perfume that was launched in 1939 as the first U.S. fragrance to compete directly with French perfumes such as Chanel No. 5. Prior to the introduction of White Shoulders, all upscale perfumes were imported. Over time and because of neglected image advertising, White Shoulders became known as a fragrance for the over-50 set. Unfortunately, demographic analysis shows that the 25–35 year olds are now the most lucrative market. The care and feeding of White Shoulders had been neglected and sales began eroding. In fact, it was often difficult to find a store that wanted to stock the product. The new owner, Chesebrough-Ponds, plans an updated image with a $6 million marketing campaign aimed at the most lucrative consumer group. The advertising will be updated along with the packaging and cameo trademark. Success in revitalizing this neglected trademark in a fiercely competitive market is not at all assured. Possibly, better care and feeding of the image along the way could have averted the deteriorating situations.

## Overexposure and Misuse

Care and feeding of a well positioned trademark must include discriminating use. Blasting a trademark across everything that doesn't move violates the traditions of trademark image and positioning. Donald Trump is a classic example of overdrive in line extensions. An article in *Advertising Age*, June 11, 1990, quoted Al Ries, chairman of the marketing specialists Trout and Ries. Ries said that "the Trump brand name, now on buildings, airlines, casinos, a board game, a book and an upcoming T.V. game show has become a joke." Initially, the name Trump stood for power and glamour. Ries indicated that "the worst thing in the world is to turn a brand name into fad . . . Trump put his name on too many things—anything that stood still for two minutes."

Part of the allure of a trademark is credibility. Customers associate product and service attributes with certain names. Ivory soap stands for purity. Volvo promises safety. Brooks Brothers means serious business. When a trademark is spread thinly across incongruous products, the attributes for which it is known get lost.

Pierre Cardin once stood for the height of fashion. The name then started to appear on off-the-rack clothing and inexpensive luggage, followed by clock radios that were given away as magazine subscription premiums. Lost forever is associating the name with upscale and expensive fashions.

The art of extending the use of a trademark into areas where it has no presence, image, or positioning can present further risks. Associating the name with too many individual economic ventures places all the products at risk if anything happens to tarnish the image of the single trademark. All the individual components can be affected in domino-like fashion. This is exactly what happened to

Trump. Cracks in the image of power and prestige affect all the businesses on which the Trump name is used. The cracks come from the potential divorce in his life and the question of financial solvency that plagues all his business dealings. The image of power and glitz fades and hurts everything.

---

Key Investment Concept #23

Overextension of a trademark can dinimish its value. When the ability to command premium prices and to dominate markets is lost, investment performance is likely to suffer. When trademark overextension is detected, it may be time to sell the stock.

---

## Unique Forms of Care and Feeding

As previously discussed in Chapter 6, the care and feeding of intangible assets can take unique forms. Polaroid has sued Kodak for infringement of patents. The damage award reached the extraordinary amount of $1 billion. The benefits to Polaroid, however, are more than just receiving a huge check.

By winning an infringement case, Polaroid has eliminated a competitor from the market. Larger sales volumes allow cost savings in manufacturing due to increased volume. Additionally, profit margins benefit from premium prices that can be enjoyed in a monopolistic environment. As previously discussed, premium pricing is not limitless. Consumers may not have many alternative instant photography choices but they still have choices among many traditional photographic products with which Polaroid must still compete. At certain price levels, Polaroid would not be able to sell any instant cameras even if no other photographic alternatives existed. However, the company still is free to test the price elasticity of the market without the presence of Kodak and higher profits are likely.

The same benefits are true for Procter & Gamble, which eliminated competitors of its crisp and chewy cookie after successfully suing infringers. Unrestricted premium pricing can be tested and fine-tuned as Procter & Gamble continues as the single source.

As we see, the care and feeding of intangible assets can take unique forms. In these cases, Procter & Gamble and Polaroid used the legal system.

### An Even Balance Is Needed

*The Wall Street Journal,* April 11, 1990, included an article entitled "How Ashton-Tate Lost Its Leadership in Personal Computer Software Arena." Ashton-Tate was once a big company in the personal computer industry, sharing the lead with Microsoft Corporation and Lotus Development Corporation. The cash cow product on which the company was built was dBASE. In fact, the product helped to accelerate the use of personal computers in the early 1980s by giving customers a flexible way of organizing and retrieving large amounts of data. Unfortunately, the company faded from the leadership position.

In early 1988, Ashton-Tate released an improved version of its cash cow product only to find that features were lacking and that the product was too slow and had an annoying tendency to crash during use. Fixing the flaws took an incredible amount of time, causing the company to lose prestige and allowing competitors to steal market share. As a result, the company has experienced slumping sales and profits that deteriorated into losses.

In an industry where high technology dominates and also where technology has a short life cycle, constant attention to technical expertise is vital. At Ashton-Tate the focus of management shifted heavily to marketing and product packaging. The lack of emphasis on technology and product development meant that the necessary care and feeding of the fragile technological edge were absent. William Davidow, venture capitalist and writer on high-technology companies, indicated that "every technology company needs a visionary who can perceive the general trend of a market . . . without one, a company very quickly loses its technology position." At Ashton-Tate the top executives became marketing oriented.

Attention shifted to diversification at Ashton-Tate. While neglecting technology, emphasis was placed on marketing and the value of the trademark. The diversification plan involved the purchase of other software products that were repackaged with the

Ashton-Tate name slapped onto the box. Unfortunately, the managers and engineers who were acquired along with the companies soon left, along with the technological care and feeding tools that were so important and desperately needed. The shift of care and feeding activities went too far in favor of supporting one intangible asset while neglecting another. A fine balance is needed. Disaster strikes when the balance becomes tilted.

## Beyond Patents and Trademarks

Other intangible assets also deteriorate but sometimes it is for reasons beyond the control of management. When a healthy bank acquires another healthy bank, avoiding situations where the S&L crisis would confuse issues, one of the primary assets that are acquired is the depositor base. This represents the amount of deposits in checking and savings accounts, certificates of deposit, and Christmas clubs. The customers that comprise the depositor base represent an intangible asset. For the most part, they are the most important intangible assets. The only other assets that are acquired with a bank are branch offices, office equipment, teller stations, and vaults. For various reasons, the customer base over time deteriorates. People die, move, go bankrupt, and withdraw deposits for major purchases such as college educations and homes. Therefore, the intangible assets of a bank as represented by the depositor base constantly need care and feeding to replenish lost depositors.

Another example is the insurance industry. A primary asset of most insurance companies is the intangible asset often described as insurance-in-force. This represents property, casualty, and life insurance policies, which represent an important portfolio of business. Through no fault of their own, insurance companies watch insurance-in-force deteriorate. Policy holders die. The policy is paid and one element of the intangible asset is gone. Over time the entire base of life insurance policies is eventually paid. Without vigilant care and feeding efforts, the intangible asset disappears completely.

Distribution networks, as previously discussed, are a very important intangible asset. They can be comprised of independent sales representatives, grocery store chains, upscale department stores, and mail order catalogs. Sales representatives die, upscale department stores go bankrupt, and mail order catalogs get lost. Without constant efforts to renew and replace distributors, over time the means of making sales will be lost completely.

In publishing, the list of book titles that have sustained continuing sales can be the most important asset owned. However, without care and feeding efforts to constantly add new titles to the list, the growth of the company is likely to cease and eventually the fresh list of titles will fade into a stale list of unsold volumes.

All intangible assets must vigilantly be maintained.

---

Key Investment Concept #24

When investing in a company that possesses a valuable portfolio of intangible assets, success is more likely if the company also possesses the mechanism to maintain, refresh, nurture, and care for these fragile assets.

---

## Diversification Is Usually Bad News

Diversification often means that the care and feeding of intangible assets are about to be neglected. The investment success of Peter Lynch, retired manager of Fidelity Magellan Fund, is legendary. Lynch refers to diversifying acquisitions as "diworsefication."[1] A long list of major companies have diversified themselves into financial trouble. General Electric has had big disappointments from its acquisition of Kidder Peabody and American Express has not been minting money with its acquisitions of Shearson Lehman and E. F. Hutton.

Managers at successful companies start to feel invincible. They begin to think that they can make money in any business they choose. Maybe management just becomes bored with the original business and starts looking for new challenges. Either way, acqui-

---

[1] Lynch, Peter, *One up on Wall Street,* Simon & Schuster, New York, 1989, p. 146

sitions outside the discipline of the original business get made and most often huge amounts of money are lost. Acquisition prices are often too high and the acquired businesses turn out to be much more complex than originally anticipated. Later, the acquired business is sold at a loss.

Saatchi & Saatchi provides a recent example. With U.K. advertising roots, the company expanded into public relations consulting. Next, advertising agencies in the United States were acquired. Management then decided that a broader range of business was the key to success and entered into an acquisition binge that included compensation consulting, executive recruiting, and intellectual property consulting. With the acquisitions completed, the company found that all consulting services are not alike. Top management couldn't understand all the different consulting disciplines and lost the senior professionals that were acquired along with many established customers. Many of the acquired businesses started to lose money.

Saatchi is now best known for its divestment *strategy* as it sells off the consulting businesses that were purchased only a few years ago. Many are being sold back to the original owners at less price than Saatchi originally paid.

More disturbing is the message behind diworsefying acquisitions. Management is saying that they have run out of new strategies for the original business. They have run out of new product ideas, cannot think of any more new ways to improve production processes, and do not know any other way to exploit established trademarks. It is more likely that the management talents have peaked and not the potential of the underlying business. Nonetheless, it is very likely that the needed care and feeding of the core business intangible assets will be neglected and perhaps even sacrificed as management's attention focuses on its new toy.

Good diversifying acquisitions are possible but they are in the minority. Other avenues of reinvestment are always available. Improvements are always possible. The growing market share of Japanese products in mature and stagnant industries proves that new product ideas, improved process techniques, and extended exploitation of trademarks are always possible. On the rare occasion where perfection has indeed been achieved by a company, stock buy-back programs or special dividend payments are more likely to raise a stock price than any diworsefication binge.

Investors should be alert to diversification announcements. They should be viewed with skepticism because the investment risk of the company has very likely just increased. The care and feeding of the core business may suffer, which then leads to deterioration of the stock price.

---

**Key Investment Concept #25**

Diversifying acquisitions should be viewed with fear. Investors should be concerned about the continued commitment to the efforts that are required to maintain and support keystone intangible assets.

---

# 8

# STRATEGIES FOR FULL EXPLOITATION

This chapter is about the future. It presents the exploitation strategies that will propel companies beyond the year 2000. Companies that incorporate one or more of these strategies will doubtless become the growth stocks for the 1990s and beyond.

Future growth and profit success will come from *licensing, joint ventures,* and *extension* of the value of intangible assets. When considering the purchase of a stock, a thorough and diligent analysis should include a review of the efforts being pursued to exploit keystone intangible assets.

The strategic exploitation of intangible assets is the next dimension of business activity. Profitability has been enhanced, perhaps even optimally, by recent efforts to cut costs, boost quality, and shower the market with customer service. With companies and their competitors optimizing cost controls and approaching customer service parity, future efforts to enhance profits must focus elsewhere in order to find a reliable leading edge that can fuel growth. The only reliable way to stay ahead of the competition is to leap into new niches and introduce next generation products and services. Intangible assets will serve in the coming decade as the spring board.

In the previous chapter overextension was discussed as very often having a deteriorating effect on the value of a trademark. In this chapter, emphasis is placed on successful strategies that extend the use of intangible assets.

## Licensing

Licensing intangible assets to others is just like leasing someone a building. All, or part, of the rights associated with the intangible asset are transferred to another party in exchange for a future stream of royalties. The royalties are usually paid as a percentage of sales that the licenser/renter derives from having access to the intangible asset.

This practice can make sense in many cases where a technology cannot easily be exploited by the owner or where the owner does not possess the funds needed to establish a strong position in the market. It is also useful when the owner does not have any management expertise in the industry to which the licensed property will be applied. Licensing allows the owner of the intangible asset to gain revenues from markets in which it would not otherwise be able to participate.

Very often licensing also allows an intangible asset owner to gain access to the intangible assets of others. Instead of licensing technology for a monetary fee, high-technology companies are trading licenses on each other's coveted technology. This practice is often pursued in the software industry.

## Technology Licensing

Alza Corporation currently earns 100% of its profits from royalty fees. The royalty fees are paid to Alza by drug companies that incorporate drug delivery systems of Alza's into their own pharmaceutical products. Royalties and fees of $8.6 million nearly match the company's pretax income for the quarter ended March 31, 1990. For the long term, the company is planning to establish its own manufacturing capabilities for use in the sale of its own products. By the year 2000, the company hopes to have income split 50–50 between manufacturing efforts and royalty payments. This is an example of how licensing can be used as the foundation on which a new company is built.

Royalty income can be a lot more then pocket change to some companies. Texas Instrument has recently decided to cash in on some of the basic patents that it has had for decades. The company owns patents on basic memory-chip technology. Security analysts estimate that the company collects about $150 million annually from royalties. The patents are important incremental patents on the basic invention that was made by Intel. Just recently, the company obtained a Japanese patent on integrated circuits. It has been speculated that the royalty fees from the integrated circuit patent could have a royalty rate of approximately 3%. Based on the $20 billion annual volume of products that have integrated circuits in Japan, royalties from this new patent could approach $600 million per year for Texas Instrument. This is solely from licensing. Manufacturing or marketing activities by Texas Instrument are not involved. Nor is any form of additional investment required. In the future, this amount of royalty could easily and substantially eclipse the importance of conducting operations, which have recently shown losses.

IBM approaches licensing from a different angle. With one of the world's largest portfolios of patents, the company broadly licenses in exchange for cross-licensing agreements that provide the company with access to the patents of other companies. Royalty income isn't as important to IBM as the opportunity to use and exploit other people's patents.

One of the big problems with licensing, however, is that it can ultimately create a formidable competitor. In many businesses, there is a trend away from licensing technology. Don Phillips, vice president of Hoechst-Celanese, explains that the future lies in joint ventures. When a license is granted, the licensing company only enjoys royalties on the patented technology for the remaining life of the patent. Depending on the licensing clauses, the period of royalty revenues can be even less. At the end of the licensing agreement or when the patent expires, the licenser may have created a new competitor. The U.S. experience with Japan is a perfect example. Initially, Japanese companies licensed technology from the United States or manufactured for U.S. companies. Eventually, Japanese companies stood on their own and now dominate many markets in the United States. In response, Don Phillips indicates that the exploitation of patents will be based more on deals and affiliations that provide a *permanent* benefit to both parties. Licensing will continue to be an important source of income and should continue to prevail in trademarks, but for patented technology a competitor is created at the end of 17 years and continued revenues vanish. As such, experts like Don Phillips expect to see more joint ventures and less licensing of technology in the future.

In market areas where the licenser does not plan to establish a strong presence, however, licensing is still a tremendous means by which to extend the economic benefits of otherwise idle technology.

## Trademark Licensing

Trademark licensing is leverage in marketing. It can represent a low cost, low risk way to add income to the licenser and expand the market potential of the licensee. Considering the astronomical costs to develop and nurture a new brand name and the scarcity of names that are available, licensing is becoming an opportunity for growth. The demand for use of well known trademarks will drive higher the royalty fees that trademarks can command.

Licensing not only provides the licenser with an additional source of income but also expands the means by which the trademark can receive exposure and publicity. Licensing is basically borrowing the established acceptance of consumers in one product area and using that acceptance in another product area. When the use of the trademark is extended through a license, the licenser receives a royalty income.

Consumer acceptance can be defined as the recognition by the consumer of the name and an affection for what the trademark represents. When a consumer finds an "old friend" trademark on a new product, that person immediately recognizes the trademark and usually extends the affection for the trademark to the new product.

The licensing of trademarks generally falls into two categories: *extension licensing* and *collateral licensing*.

Extension licensing refers to the use of a trademark on products that are a natural or logical extension of well known and trusted core products. The motivation to buy the licensed product is based on the reputation of the core trademark and all the desirable qualities and characteristics for which it stands. In many instances, the extended use is so close and so natural that consumers may be unaware that the product is produced by a licensee.

Collateralized licensing refers to the use of a trademark on products that have little or no apparent connection with the core trademark. Examples include Budweiser beach towels, Porsche sunglasses, and Harley Davidson beer. The motivation to buy the product when collaterally licensed is driven by the recognizability of the core brand and the desire on the consumer's part to express association with the n ime and all that it stands for.

The advantages to the licenser include royalty income and enhanced advertising. Income is derived from royalties on the sales of the products that use the trademark. Enhanced advertising comes from the visibility that the trademark enjoys. "Cool dudes" lounging on the beach covered with Budweiser blankets complements the core advertising program of the company.

Trademark licensing can be an important source of revenue and is not to be overlooked if the exploitation of well known trademarks is to be achieved. It is important, however, that a licensed program adheres to the care and feeding standards previously discussed. The use of a well known trademark on inferior quality products can tarnish the reputation of the name and affect sales of the core products. Also, in order to be successful, the licensing program should be limited to areas where the name has credibility. It is unlikely that a line of clothing with the Kaopectate name will have much success.

Trademark licensing contributes more then $60 billion annually to retail sales in volume of goods and services in the United States. Exhibit 8-1 shows the percentage of licensed merchandise at the retail level:

A trend in licensing is currently toward classic characters and trademarks. America is going back to traditional values, back to the days of the *nuclear* family. Consequently, demand for classic names like the Flintstones, Peanuts, Mickey Mouse, and Campbell Soup is increasing. Nostalgia sells and traditional names are the most valuable intangible assets in the current market.

*Exhibit 8-1*   Sales of Licensed Trademarks

| Product Category | Percentage |
|---|---|
| Apparel and accessories | 35.5% |
| Toys and games | 12.0% |
| Publishing/stationery | 10.5% |
| Gifts and novelties | 10.0% |
| Home furnishings/housewares | 10.5% |
| Sporting goods | 3.0% |
| Foods and beverages | 8.0% |
| Health and beauty aids | 5.0% |
| Electronics | 5.0% |
| Other | 0.5% |
| Total | $64.6    billion |

Consumers are becoming better informed and more particular. Trademark licensing as a result is being done in a much more thoughtful manner. Licensers can no longer slap a logo onto any product and enjoy long-term profitability. Credibility is the key. It must be present when extending trademarks or its cachet may be diluted.

Proper licensing extends the use of a trademark without overextending it. In the case of Dr. Scholl's, the trademark is extended to areas where it can remain credible. The company is long known for providing footwear comfort. Licensing and extension of the trademark have therefore been limited to hosiery, footwear, shoes, and electric foot massagers.

Legal control of trademarks is infinite and involves less competitive risk than the risk involved with licensing technology. A license of patented technology can eventually create a competitor. Trademark licensing is less likely to establish a new competitor.

## Licensing Benefits

Some of the benefits from licensing technology include the following:

1. An additional source of income from unused technology.
2. An opportunity to trade intellectual property for patents that would otherwise be unavailable.

3. An opportunity to participate in a market in which the company has little expertise.

4. Establishment of a foundation on which to create a new company.

5. A chance to exploit technology where adequate commercialization funds are lacking.

Some of the benefits from licensing trademarks include the following:

1. An additional source of income from unused trademarks.

2. An additional source of income from collateralized application of the name on novel products.

3. An additional source of advertising exposure associated with use on collateralized products.

4. A foundation on which to establish market positions in new industries.

## Joint Ventures

An article in *The Wall Street Journal*, August 28, 1990, was entitled "Merck and DuPont Ally to Form Drug Joint Venture." The hugely successful Merck & Company is planning the establishment of a joint venture company with DuPont. The new company will be owned on a 50–50 basis with DuPont contributing its entire pharmaceutical operation, which is expected to have sales for the year 1990 of $550 million. Merck will provide foreign marketing rights to sell some of its prescription medicine plus an undisclosed amount of cash. The chairman and chief executive officer of Merck, Roy Bagellos, said "We're convinced that we have to increase our access to R&D if we want to increase our worldwide market share." The combination gives Merck access to experimental drugs that are currently being developed by DuPont. The research department at Merck is widely acclaimed as one of the best in the pharmaceutical industry, yet management officials at Merck say that in order to remain a premium growth company outside help in developing new technology is needed. The benefit for DuPont will be access to the foreign sales expertise that is possessed by Merck. Joseph Mollica, a DuPont vice president, said: "We realize that if we ever are going to make it as a drug company we need to be able to sell our new products in foreign markets." This joint venture is an example of two companies gaining access to the valuable intangible assets of the other company. *Merck gets access to new drug technology and DuPont gets the benefits of a well established sales force.*

## The Essence of Joint Ventures

Two independent business entities can gain permanent access to the proprietary intangible assets of another through joint ventures. Many benefits are involved.

Most important is that access to the intangible assets can be obtained without the uncertainty associated with internal development (failure to achieve successful development) and can be obtained faster than internal development would allow.

A company that desires the intangible assets of another can acquire the entire company that possesses the desired assets. Problems can arise, however, from the financial burden involved. The desired intangible assets may be obtained but the acquisition debt may preclude using funds to exploit the coveted intangible assets. Another problem with acquisitions is that the contingent liabilities of the acquired company come along whether wanted or not.

Access to specific proprietary intangible assets is possible through joint ventures without having to acquire an entire company. By pooling specific intangible assets and resources into an independent joint venture, many companies in the future will enjoy full exploitation of their technological assets.

Independent joint venture benefits include the following:

1.  Focused management on the strategies of the new venture.
2.  Freedom from incompatible corporate cultures that may prevail at the parent firms but that may be inappropriate for the industry in which the new venture operates.
3.  Limited liability for the venture partners.
4.  An independent financial structure for the new entity free of the parent firms and unencumbering to the parents.

5. Specific integration of selected intangible assets that are complementary according to a well developed plan that addresses a specific market.

6. Permanent participation by all joint venture parties in the profits of the new enterprise.

Even the U.S. government is getting into the act. The Defense Department is investing for the first time in a small company, which effectively represents a joint venture. Gazelle Micro-circuits Incorporated will be receiving $4 million from the Defense Department to develop ultra-high-speed data communications projects. In exchange, for the investment, the Defense Department is expected to receive a fair return on the investment similar to the that which is received by venture capitalists for investments in companies that possess important technology. The Defense Department has the alternative of taking royalties on sales instead of common stock. Traditionally, the government has funded research and development projects by grants and contracts. The new trend is for the government funding to entitle the Defense Department to the rewards of joint venture investment. The trend for joint ventures in the future is absolutely clear. When the slow moving bureaucratic government of the United States gets involved, the benefits must be exceedingly clear.

*The Wall Street Journal*, September 13, 1989, contained an article entitled "United Technologies and Dow Chemical Plan Joint Venture." The two companies announced that they signed a letter of understanding to form a joint venture involving the manufacturing and sale of aerospace, defense, and automotive parts. The parts will be made of composite materials. The combination will couple Dow Chemical's advanced composite fabrication technology with the composite parts manufacturing operations of United Technologies' Sikorski Aircraft division. The agreement states that Dow will provide growth capital, research, polymer and fabrication technology along with certain patent licenses. United Technologies will contribute to the venture Sikorski's existing composite parts and production facility in Alabama. In addition, United Technologies will provide engineering and research from its Connecticut facility along with some contracts that it has for parts. All are important intangible assets that give the new entity a tremendous advantage over any other kind of start-up company. Eugene Buckley, president of Sikorski Aircraft, said: "After careful analysis of the projected growth in this market we concluded that the effort merited the focus of a new company and that its joint venture with a major leader in composite parts was the way to go."

Joint ventures allow each party to enjoy the intangible asset advantages possessed by the other partner. In addition, the independent entity is free to operate unencumbered by the bureaucracy of the two parent companies. The new company is therefore more focused than it might otherwise be as a division of one of the founding joint partner members.

Joint ventures are going to be a fundamental strategy for the exploitation of technology. Companies that implement this strategy properly will expand their sources of earnings. These are the companies that represent the best stock investment opportunities.

## Extension

Extensions are the use of intangible assets by the owner for its own expansion into new areas. Extension can be viewed as a form of internal licensing and is typically accomplished without a joint venture partner. The following list shows how some trademarks have successfully been extended.

- Coppertone, long known for suntanning products, has introduced a line of sunglasses. They are sold at the same convenient locations that suntanning lotions are located and are geared toward the beach crowd.
- Flintstones, well known by children as a popular cartoon character, has introduced a line of vitamins and snack foods that are aimed at children.
- Dr. Scholl's has long provided foot comfort and eased foot odor with the sale of foot-pad inserts that it has sold for decades. The company has recently introduced a line of athletic socks, shoes, and foot massagers.

○ Campbell Soup recently placed its good name on kitchen utensils and on a line of children's kitchen toys. The kitchen toys for children are expected to establish brand loyalty with children long before they ever become shoppers.

One of the best extenders of intangible assets is Disney. In *The Wall Street Journal,* an article entitled "Disney Aims to Become Big in Books for Little People" described how the company plans to use its name in the publishing business. Past success of the company from establishing its own record label has stirred interest at the company to enter the booming market for children's books rather than just continuing to license other publishers. Three publishing units are planned by the company. Disney Press is planned to publish books that are based on Disney characters and movies. Muppet Press is expected to publish books for children using the Muppet characters. An additional imprint "yet unnamed" will publish high-quality juvenile books independent of Disney and Muppet characters.

The power of extending the Disney and Muppet names into publishing has obvious attributes when considering the recognizability and affection that are already established with loyal customers. A further and significant advantage involves the ability of Disney to lure away top artists and writers. Brenda Bowen, editor and chief of juvenile books for Henry Holt and Company, indicated: "Our fear is that Disney money will lure away top artists and writers. Maybe they will promise to make their books into movies."

The competition in the children's book business is very crowded but the Disney name has more marketing muscle and greater recognition with children and parents then any other company in the world. In addition to exploitation of the Disney name and all the famous characters, another intangible asset that will neatly be exploited includes the Disney stores that are spread across 25 states in upscale shopping malls. Also, the company will be able to promote children's books in its new magazine for children entitled *Disney Adventures.* The magazine is a revitalization of a publication that has not been printed for 50 years.

Another classic that is being extended is Barbie. Initially, this doll was the only product of the business. Quickly, Barbie outfits hit the market, followed by other accessories such as toy cars, houses, and furniture. Now from the people that bring you Bran Chex and Wheat Chex a new, sweet, fruit flavored cereal that is shaped like hearts, bows, stars, and cars will feature the Barbie name. In addition, Barbie has been exploited by having the name applied to a new line of girls' clothing as well as bed linens and bathroom towels with Barbie motifs.

An article entitled "Tea, Sympathy and Direct Mail" appeared in *Forbes* in the September 19, 1989 issue. The article described how Marriott is planning to become the leader in the business of hybrid retirement/nursing homes. The company conducted a mass mailing that offered charter memberships in its new Jefferson Condominium.

Management plans to provide maid service, a health club, 24 hour emergency call buttons, communal meals, skilled nursing rooms, and services such as "assisted living" for those that don't need continual care but need assistance with some activities like dressing. Response from the direct mail was an outstanding 4%. Typically, in the direct mail business, 2% is considered very good. A 4% response rate is extraordinary. The demographic trend for the future will make retirement communities big business.

The industry as described by *Forbes* "has more than its fair share of sleazy operators." Marriott found that it has one very important marketing advantage: its good name. One of the respondents that paid the $1000 deposit was interviewed and said: "We felt Marriott would do things in a nice manner." James Eden, Senior Living Services general manager, said: "One of the things that has been inherently wrong with this business over the past years is that it has been more of a developer driven business than a consumer driven business."

The retirement/nursing home service is difficult to sell. Customers that make an investment in such a project, even a down payment, are admitting that they are becoming frailer and older. People are reluctant to think about the inevitability of their own decay. When the reputation of the industry is introduced into the equation, it is easy to understand why many people put off the decision indefinitely. Marriott sees an opportunity and its trademark stands for *quality*. Not only will the application of the Marriott trademark to the nursing home industry likely be profitable for the company, it may have the added benefit of revolutionizing the industry.

## Extending Technology

"Sony Draws a New Toy" is an article that appeared in *Advertising Age* on March 19, 1990. Beginning in 1987, Sony launched a new product line that took it into the toy market. The "My First Sony" line introduced quality radios and tape players for kids. In addition, the company is selling electronic sketch pads that display the drawings of children on television screens. Unlike many of the electronic products sold to children, Sony products are reliable, sturdy, and possess high-quality characteristics. The extension of the Sony technology into the toy market not only provides the company with another source of sales but also plants the seeds with consumers at a young age for the development of loyal customers.

In *The New York Times*, February 25, 1990, an article entitled "A Radical New Style for Old Gillette" discusses how the company is using its famous trademark to introduce a technologically advanced "super blade." Most of the advances in the slow-moving world of razors have relied on metal coatings on the razor blade and lubricating strips. A new product about to be introduced by Gillette, currently being tested in Europe, has a significant mechanical advantage. The new product is called *Sensor* and it took about $200 million to develop. The new product involves tin blades that are laser welded and mounted on springs. According to Gillette, a better shave is the result. Gillette has operations in toiletries, stationery products, electric appliances, and toothbrushes. The profit margins are strong in almost every segment but razor blades are estimated to have profit margins that are more then twice that of any of the other operating divisions. In the stagnant market for men's shaving equipment, Gillette is locked in a battle for market share with Bic and Warner-Lambert's Schick. By placing the Gillette name on the first new technology introduced in the shaving market in 13 years, the company hopes to break out of its stagnant share of the market and use the combination of new technology and an established trademark to expand its business.

## Unique Exploitation Strategy

In *The New York Times,* January 14, 1990, article entitled "A White Knight Draws Cries of Patent Blackmail," a unique form of intellectual property exploitation is discussed. The Refac Technology Development Corporation is based in New York City. The company promotes itself as a "white knight" that assists small inventors by providing them with resources to fight legal battles against giant infringers. Critics charge that the company makes millions of dollars through "patent blackmail" and manipulation of weaknesses that exist in the patent system. Whether or not the critics are correct, the company exploits intellectual property in a unique form by using patent infringement lawsuits. The company has filed 2000 infringement cases and has another 1000 additional filings under consideration. Targets of the company include IBM, Eastman Kodak, R. H. Macy's, Sears, and Radio Shack.

The company currently acquires patents that have been infringed upon and then initiates infringement lawsuits. By negotiating settlements and/or royalty licenses, the company recently enjoyed $10.2 million for the first 9 months of 1989 as royalty income. The company also enjoys a 25% after-tax profit margin.

Refac was founded in 1952 by Eugene M. Lang as a licensing company. Typically, the company acquires a patent in exchange for assuming the responsibilities for negotiating royalties or promising to litigate if necessary. Royalty income is typically split with the inventors from whom the patent was obtained.

The chief executive of Refac, Eugene M. Lang, came to national celebrity after devising a program with a class of Harlem sixth graders. The deal involved a promise that any of the students that finished high school would be guaranteed money to cover college expenses. Mr. Lang continues to defend the "little guy" inventor as they battle against the giant infringers.

Some of the basic patents that the company owns include:

Liquid crystal displays
Automatic teller machines
Credit verification systems

Bar code scanning systems
Video cassette recorders
Electronic keyboards
Spreadsheet software

Tactics at Refac can be viewed as exploitation of the legal system but they are still based on the power and value of intangible assets such as patents.

## Compelling Reasons to Exploit

The 1980s were a period of exceptional changes in Europe, where merges and acquisitions (M&A) took a leading role in the construction of the European industry. While M&A continue to make the headlines, a range of other strategies, including cross-border-alliances, cross shareholdering, and joint purchasing, are underway in anticipation of the opportunities that the Europe of 1992 will offer. To capitalize on these opportunities and to avoid being edged out by aggressive competition, companies are redefining their growth strategies and are looking for new ways to gain competitive advantage. The race for a unified economic Europe has fueled the fire for joint ventures and licensing projects. Licensing, joint ventures, and product extension are not limited to the United States. As an example, Mickey Mouse books sold like hotcakes in Moscow at $2.40 per copy with 200,000 copies sold out as fast as they hit the shelves. The complete sellout occurred in only a few hours. On the news of such success, Disney stock increased $6 per share.

## Leading Edge Opportunities

Established intangible assets are no longer being overlooked as companies attempt to grow. Gone are the days of acquiring any business that looks like fun. Thoughtful strategies that are based on exploiting technology, trademarks, and copyrights will be the hallmark of successful companies in the future and the stuff of which winning stocks are made.

---

### Key Investment Concept #26

Winning stocks of the future will be those of companies that pursue licensing, joint ventures, and extension of intangible assets.

---

# 9

# ONLY SHADOWS OF INTANGIBLE ASSETS ARE FOUND IN ACCOUNTING STATEMENTS

The financial statements of a business "are prepared as a medium of communication between a business entity and interested parties."[1] Unfortunately, in the majority of cases the most important assets that a company can own are wholly absent. Most often, intangible assets aren't even mentioned in a footnote.

For investors, the financial statements are the primary source of information about a company. Messages from the executive man-

---

[1] Michael G. Tearney, "Accounting for Goodwill: A Realistic Approach," *The Journal of Accountancy*, July 1973, p. 43.

agement usually begin each financial report followed by the income statement, which measures profit performance for the past year. The balance sheet then follows with the assets of the company and the liabilities. These financial reports also very often present background information about company products and markets. A large number of institutional and individual investors rely on the accounting statements of companies. From these statements critical opinions about financial condition, stability, growth prospects, and profitability are formed. From these statements important decisions are made about the potential for investment performance.

Throughout this book, intangible assets have been shown as the primary source of investment performance. The intangible assets that have been discussed represent the spark plug of the business enterprise engine. These assets are the difference between suffering with the mediocre performance of a commodity business or basking in the stellar performance of a proprietary business domain. In some cases, the intangible assets owned by a company are more valuable than the combined value of all other property. Billions are spent to create trademarks and billions are spent to develop technology. Yet, accounting statements cannot find a way to incorporate these keystone assets into the principal source of information that is used by all investors.

In this chapter, the substantial weaknesses of intangible asset accounting are exposed and other sources of information that can help fill the gap are identified.

## Financial Statements

The financial statements of a business enterprise are intended to provide (1) a "snapshot" of the assets and liabilities of the business at a specific point in time (balance sheet) and (2) a summary of the transactions of the past year (income statement). These statements are fundamental to security analysts, portfolio managers, bankers, pension fund managers, and individual investors. They represent the financial condition of the business and show its record of achieving profitability.

## Balance Sheet

The two primary elements of the balance sheet are *assets* and *liabilities*. The characteristics of these elements are described in *Statement of Financial Accounting Concepts No. 6*, published by the Financial Accounting Standards Board (FASB).

## Assets

Accounting elements that are to be included on the asset side of the balance sheet are described as follows:

Assets are probable future economic benefits obtained or controlled by a particular entity as a result of past transactions or events.[2]

An asset has three essential characteristics:(a) it embodies a probable future benefit that involves a capacity, singly or in combination with other assets, to contribute directly or indirectly to future net cash inflows, (b) a particular entity can obtain the benefit and control others' access to it, and (c) the transaction or other event giving rise to the entity's right to or control of the benefit has already occurred."[3]

The common characteristic possessed by all assets (economic resources) is "service potential" or "future economic benefit," the scarce capacity to provide services or benefits to the entities that use them. In a business enterprise, that service potential or future economic benefit eventually results in net cash inflows to the enterprise.[4]

Once acquired, an asset continues as an asset of the entity until the entity collects it, transfers it to another entity, or uses it up, or some other event or circumstance destroys the future benefit or removes the entity's ability to obtain it.[5]

---

[2] Financial Accounting Standards Board, *Statement of Financial Accounting Concepts No.6*, 1985, p. 10.
[3] See footnote, p. 10
[4] See footnote 2, p. 11.
[5] See footnote 2, p. 12.

Basically, anything that is already owned by a company, lasts for more than one accounting year, directly delivers future economic benefits, and can be controlled exclusively by a business can be classified on a balance sheet as an asset. Unfortunately, this broad FASB definition of assets is rarely used to the fullest extent possible, and therefore the admirable objectives of financial statements are never fully achieved.

## Liabilities

The accounting elements described as liabilities of the business have been addressed as follows:

> Liabilities are probable future sacrifices of economic benefits arising from present obligations of a particular entity to transfer assets or provide services to other entities in the future as a result of past transactions or events.[6]

Liabilities are the debts of the company. Current liabilities are debts that must be satisfied within the current accounting year. All other liabilities are characterized as long term, to be satisfied in future years. Together with the funds that were originally contributed by investors, the liability funds are used to acquire and maintain the assets of the business.

## Shareholders' Equity

Shareholders' equity is defined as follows:

> The equity or net assets of . . . a business enterprise . . . is the difference between the entity's assets and its liabilities. It is a residual, affected by all events that increase or decrease total assets by different amounts than they increase or decrease total liabilities.[7]

In a business enterprise, the equity is the ownership interest.[8]

---

[6] See footnote 2, p. 13.
[7] See footnote 2, p. 17.
[8] See footnote 2, p. 20.

| *Exhibit 9-1* Layout of Balance Sheet | |
| --- | --- |
| Assets | Liabilities |
| Current assets | Current liabilities |
| Plant, property, and equipment | Long-term debt |
| Other assets | Shareholders' equity |

Exhibit 9-1 displays the layout of a common balance sheet.

Total assets are comprised of current assets, tangible assets, and other assets. Current assets are those that can be converted to cash or used in operations during the next 12 months. Inventories and accounts receivable are the most common and typically the largest component of current assets.

Tangible assets are typically described as "plant, property, and equipment" or "fixed assets." The accounting elements are in three parts: the original cost of the property is shown, together with depreciation or amortization reserves and the amount of "net plant."

The "other assets" category is usually a minor account for assets such as prepaid expenses, minority interests in other businesses, and long-term assets that are not used directly in business operations.

## Accounting for Assets

The capitalization policy of fixed assets addresses the question of which expenditures should be treated as current expenses and which should be capitalized. The process of capitalization is the basis on which costs are allocated to future time periods. As an example, an expenditure for office supplies is treated as a current expense because it is reasonable to expect that the supplies will be used up within a few months or a year. It is therefore logical that the current operations of the business bear the expense. A building provides service to the business for a long time and it is appropriate to allocate the purchase or construction cost of the structure over a number of years. The cost of the building is therefore capitalized as an asset on the balance sheet. The mechanism for making the allocation of asset costs to accounting periods has been called depreciation. This concept is very well described by the FASB:

The goal of accrual accounting is to account in the periods in which they occur for the effects on an entity of transactions and other events and circumstances, to the extent that those financial effects are recognizable and measurable.[9]

Many assets yield their benefits to an entity over several periods, for example, prepaid insurance, buildings, and various kinds of equipment. Expenses resulting from their use are normally allocated to the periods of their estimated useful lives (the periods over which they are expected to provide benefits) by a "systematic and rational" allocation procedure, for example, by recognizing depreciation or other amortization.[10]

In this way there is a matching of revenues and expenses and the cost of capitalized assets is allocated over the periods in which those assets are useful to the business. The accumulated depreciation or capital recovery reserve is the accumulation of those periodic expense allocations and represents a reduction to the original cost of an asset.

## Accounting for Intangible Property

Accountants have long grappled with how to treat the cost of intangible property in financial statements.

When the manager of a business makes an expenditure, it must be accounted for in some fashion. If an expenditure is used to purchase a machine, the path is clear: the cost is capitalized as an asset on the balance sheet and is depreciated (charged as an expense to income) over some period of useful life. When the expenditure is used to pay an employee, it is equally clear that it represents a payment for services rendered currently and should be accounted for as an expense of the current fiscal year.

If, however, an expenditure was for research or advertising programs, the answer may not be so clear. The essential question is whether the expenditure created an asset that will provide some

---

[9] See footnote 2, p. 17.
[10] See footnote 2, p. 20.

benefit to the enterprise beyond the current period. Obsessive interpretations of accounting definitions, however, rarely allow capitalization of anything but fixed assets. The accounting profession is hesitant to categorize these expenses as having created an asset that will provide "probable future benefits."

> Coca-Cola is one of the best-recognized trademarks in the world, but it's not on their books. It got that recognition through advertising; but you don't book advertising as an asset, because you don't know if it will have future value.[11]

Neither will anyone find the technology patents on the balance sheet that built the $2 billion Polaroid Corporation. Patent infringement cost Kodak $1 billion in damages because of the value and power of the patented technological assets that are owned by Polaroid. The accounting profession, however, still isn't quite sure that internally developed intangible assets should be valued on balance sheets.

## Two Major Flaws

The most fundamental accounting principle requires that the total value of the assets equals the total amount of liabilities plus the amount of shareholders' equity. The balance sheet relationship is as follows:

$$\text{Total assets} = \text{Total liabilities} + \text{Shareholders' Equity}$$

The absence of adequate representation of the value of intangible assets directly affects the validity of the balance sheet and the income statement as follows:

1.  On the balance sheet the absence of intangible assets understates the value of shareholders' equity. By omitting intangible assets, the accounting goal of reporting all assets that will contribute future economic benefits is lost.

---

[11] Richard Green, "Inequitable Equity," *Forbes*, July 11, 1988, p. 88.

2.  On the income statement, the absence of intangible asset amorti-
    zation directly understates net income. By charging the current
    income period with trademark and patent expenses, the goal of
    matching revenues and expenses is violated and the current
    period income is charged with expenses that will benefit many
    future periods.

## Users of Accounting Reports

The failure to recognize intangible assets by the accounting profession has attracted attention from those who use financial statements.
This attraction and interest were analyzed in a research study published by the National Association of Accountants, entitled *Financial
Reporting for Security Investment and Credit Decisions*, authored by
Morton Backer. The purpose of the study was to determine the
extent to which standard accounting reports are effective in assisting
decision-making. Interviews were conducted with security analysts,
commercial bankers (loan officers), and company management.

The essence of security analysis is forecasting the probable return from a securities investment. The analyst attempts to make
qualitative judgments about a subject company's management, research and development activities, technology, patents, and trademarks, as well as studies of past financial and market performance.
Backer notes that "financial analysts frequently use the term *quality
of earnings* to describe a qualitative modification of quantified estimates of earnings for a company." They therefore are concerned
about "practices such as expensing R&D" and methods of accounting for start-up costs, market development costs, and other
items that require a decision as to whether to defer or immediately
expense.

The study also notes that analysts are relatively uninterested in
the property accounts as stated on the balance sheet. Security analysts are interested in estimating future cash flow performance. The
historical cost of fixed assets is not useful. More interesting would be
information about the current replacement cost of fixed assets. As
sales growth is forecast, the information would be useful in calculat-
ing the amounts that will be needed for reinvestment in capital
expenditures. Even more interesting would be information about the

intangible assets that have been shown to generate the largest share of earnings. At least a list that identifies them would be helpful.

Bankers, according to the study, rely on financial statements to a great extent. They too, however, do not place material weight on the property accounts or deferred charges that appear on the balance sheet. They know that the net book value of fixed assets is rarely a reflection of their market value. They also consider that intangible assets such as goodwill or other deferred charges will have no value outside the business if the need to liquidate the company becomes necessary. They are interested in seeing intangible assets on the balance sheet so that they can be distinguished and ignored. In the years since this study was prepared, there has been a significant change in the makeup of American business with the emergence of enterprises that are totally dependent on intangible assets for their existence. These businesses, just like those that were once dominated by fixed assets, require debt financing. The banking community has become much more aware of the quantity and quality of intangible assets when making loan decisions. Two of the biggest money centers in New York City regularly consider the value of well known trademarks as loan collateral. However, all too often the accounting reports do not provide enough information for use in this regard.

---

Key Investment Concept #27

The absence of intangible assets in accounting systems directly understates the value of shareholders' equity on the balance sheet and understates the amount of profits on the income statement.

---

## Acquisition Accounting Principles Make Matters Worse

The "merger mania" of the late 1960s caused a careful reexamination of the whole subject of accounting for intangibles. As business executives directed resources into acquisitions, the accounting profession and the Securities and Exchange Commission (SEC) were forced to face the issue to prevent what they perceived as a potential for misleading financial statements. Unfortunately, the results of these good intentions have provided an accounting system that is atrociously inconsistent with regard to the treatment of intangible assets. Internally developed trademarks, patents, copyrights, and other intangibles are not presented on balance sheets. When the exact same assets, however, are acquired by another company as part of a corporate takeover or merger, the intangible assets are prominently displayed on the combined balance sheet of the merged entities.

When intangible assets are acquired as part of a business combination, Opinions 16 and 17 of the Accounting Principles Board (of the American Institute of Certified Public Accountants) are controlling. These 1970 opinions, commonly referred to as APB 16 and APB 17, cover many issues related to the purchase of one company by another, and how such a business combination should be reflected on the books of the surviving business. Briefly stated, APB 16 provides that an acquisition of a business enterprise can be accounted for as a "pooling of interests" or as a "purchase."

In a *pooling,* the recorded assets and liabilities of the companies become the recorded assets and liabilities of the combined corporation at the historical cost-basis amounts of the separate companies. The accounting values that were shown on the balance sheet of the target company before the acquisition are the same values that are absorbed into the balance sheet of the acquiring company. Intangible assets will not appear on the new balance sheet unless they were already stated on the balance sheet of the acquired company prior to the transaction. For the most part, intangible assets will not be represented when acquisitions are recorded by the pooling method.

Accounting for an acquisition treated as a *purchase* is similar to that of acquiring a single asset except that the price of the entire business enterprise is attributed to different asset categories. The total price for the acquisition is allocated to:

Net working capital
Fixed assets
Intangible assets
Goodwill

When an intangible asset is purchased separately from a business combination, the price is recorded as the value of the asset. When specifically identifiable intangible assets are purchased as part of a business acquisition, a portion of the total price is allocated to intangible assets and recorded on the balance sheet. Changing the decision about how to record the acquisition can mean the difference between showing or omitting intangible assets on balance sheets.

## An Inconsistent Mess

When an acquisition is treated as a purchase rather than a pooling, intangible assets will be placed on the balance sheet at a value represented by a portion of the price paid for the acquired business.

When an acquisition is treated as a pooling of interests, intangible assets will not be identified on the opening balance sheet of the surviving company. But if the acquired company had intangible assets prior to the merger, the historical basis of the intangible assets will be placed on the opening balance sheet.

When a company uses funds to acquire an intangible asset independent of an ongoing enterprise, the price paid for the asset will be presented on the balance sheet as the basis of the acquired independent intangible asset.

When a company internally develops trademarks, patents, copyrights, and other extraordinary intangible assets, the funds expended are not capitalized and intangible assets do not appear on the balance sheet.

Financial analysis has become infinitely more complicated, especially when trying to make comparisons among competitors within an industry. Some balance sheets may show intangible assets that were acquired in an acquisition but omit intangible assets that were internally developed. Some balance sheets will not show any intangible assets at all.

The failure of accounting practices to adequately reflect intangible assets and intellectual property nearly always *understates*—in some cases dramatically—the amount of investor equity. In a recent article, Alfred Rappaport, an accounting professor at Northwestern University, is quoted as saying: "As we become a more information-intensive society, shareholder's equity is getting further away from the way the market will value a company."[12] More succinctly put, as the vital assets of business become more intangible, accounting statements become more erroneous and less useful.

## King World Productions, Inc.

King World was the first company in history to be syndicator of three simultaneous top-rated television shows—*Wheel of Fortune, Jeopardy,* and *The Oprah Winfrey Show.* The company also distributes *Inside Edition.* Revenues reached $396.4 million in 1989. Net income, after tax, totaled $76.1 million, representing an unbelievable net profit margin of 19% on sales.

Revenues are earned by the company from license fees that the company is able to get from the television stations that run the shows. The license fees go to the producers of these shows and King World keeps a percentage for being, in effect, a broker. Usually the syndicator gets one-third of the fees. As a syndicator the company is essentially a middleman; an exclusive agent who represents the producers of the various shows to the 700 network affiliated and independent television stations across the nation. The company has negotiated multi-year renewals for the shows running to 1993. Aggregate license fees for the period are expected to total almost $1 billion. If the company were to halt all other business efforts, it would still enjoy its aggregate commission on $1 billion during the next 3 years.

The rights to distribute shows come about by negotiation, outright purchase, or development of its own programs. The terms under which the company obtains the right to distribute programming varies. In agreements with Merv Griffin Enterprises (*Wheel of Fortune* and *Jeopardy*), King World is the exclusive distributor for the series as long as King World obtains sufficient broadcast commitments from television stations to cover production and distribution costs of the producer. Similarly, the company has obtained from Harpo (*The Oprah Winfrey Show*) exclusive rights to represent its

---

[12] See footnote 11.

show through the 1992–1993 season. Also, as the producer of *Inside Edition*, the company inherently owns the associated distribution rights.

In the late 1970s, King World purchased from Merv Griffin Enterprises the exclusive right to represent an evening version of *Wheel of Fortune* for $50,000. Some of the other distribution rights may have no cost basis at all, other than the negotiation efforts of company personnel. On the balance sheet the distribution agreements are not represented at all or are shown at the nominal amounts spent to acquire them, that is, $50,000 for *Wheel of Fortune*. Yet, almost 90% of the $396.4 million of revenues in 1989 came from the fees associated with these distribution agreement intangible assets.

The key asset of King World is its program portfolio: more specifically, the distribution rights that it possesses with regard to *Wheel of Fortune, Jeopardy, The Oprah Winfrey Show,* and *Inside Edition*. In addition, its program library includes films and television programs for *Sherlock Holmes, the East Side Kids, Mr. Moto, Charlie Chan, Topper, Branded, The Little Rascals,* and *The Guns of Will Sonnett*.

The balance sheet of King World is presented in Exhibit 9-2.

The balance sheet of King World includes all the different problems associated with the intangible asset inconsistent accounting mess. Yet the statements are considered by the accounting profession to represent fairly the financial condition of the company. In fact, the company is in better condition than the balance sheet shows.

It is highly likely that three of the most important elements of the balance sheet assets are inadequately represented:

Licenses and program rights
Long-term licenses and program rights
Film and video masters

The current and long-term Licenses and Program Rights refer to the exclusive distribution agreements that King World possesses. The aggregate amount associated with these assets is approximately $7.3 million. This includes the rights to distribute *The Oprah Winfrey Show, Wheel of Fortune, Jeopardy,* and other television programs. While this amount represents the cost basis of the license rights, it can hardly be

| King World Productions, Inc. | August 31, 1989 | 1988 |
|---|---|---|
| **ASSETS** | | |
| Cash and Equivalents | 47,210 | 21,311 |
| Accounts Receivable | 98,654 | 65,574 |
| Licenses and Program Rights | 2,104 | 0 |
| Advances to Producers and Others | 6,738 | 2,498 |
| Other Current Assets | 850 | 556 |
| Total Current Assets | 155,556 | 89,939 |
| Long–term Accounts Receivable | 581 | 933 |
| Long–term License and Program Rights | 5,753 | 2,976 |
| Fixed Assets: | | |
| Land, Buildings and Improvements | 4,831 | 959 |
| Broadcast Equipment | 4,535 | 0 |
| Furniture and Office Equipment | 5,202 | 3,000 |
| Film and Videotape Masters | 1,212 | 1,170 |
| Total Gross Fixed Assets | 15,780 | 5,129 |
| Less, Accumulated Depreciation and Amortization | (3,701) | (2,431) |
| Net Fixed Assets | 12,079 | 2,698 |
| Other Assets: | | |
| Goodwill and Other Intangible Assets | 112,928 | 0 |
| Advances to Producers and Others | 15,000 | 20,000 |
| Other Noncurrent Assets | 305 | 184 |
| Total Other Assets | 128,233 | 20,184 |
| TOTAL ASSETS | 302,202 | 116,730 |
| **LIABILITIES AND STOCKHOLDERS' EQUITY** | | |
| Accounts Payable and Accrued Liabilities | 6,711 | 4,476 |
| Payable to Producers and Others | 82,174 | 62,341 |
| Program Rights Payable | 1,887 | 0 |
| Income Taxes Payable, current and deferred | 31,908 | 24,701 |
| Total Current Liabilities | 122,680 | 91,518 |
| Program Rights Payable | 2,574 | 0 |
| Long–term Debt | 89,525 | 30,000 |
| Deferred Income Taxes | 25,147 | 2,420 |
| Stockholders' Equity | 62,276 | (7,208) |
| TOTAL LIABILITIES AND STOCKHOLDERS' EQUITY | 302,202 | 116,730 |

*Exhibit 9-2* King World Productions, Inc. Consolidated Balance Sheet (in thousands)

considered even remotely akin to the value of these assets. These are the assets that are responsible for 90% of 1989 revenues—$356 million. These are the same assets that are involved in multi-year renewal contracts that represent $1 billion of aggregate licensing fees. A further complication involves the rights to distribute *Inside Edition*. These licensing rights are not represented at all on the balance sheet. Since the company developed the *Inside Edition* program internally, it inherently owns the distribution rights. As such, a direct payment was never made to obtain the distribution rights and no asset for *Inside Edition* licensing rights is included. The primary assets of King World are poorly represented on the balance sheet of this company.

Film and Videotape Masters represent 68 feature films and 210 television programs that were previously identified. The cost basis for these assets totals $1.2 million. An investor is ill-advised to rely on this amount as anything approaching value. A portion of the $1.2 million is associated with the 1964 acquisition of *The Little Rascals*. Historical costs rarely contain any value elements of intangible assets. A true value of these assets would consider the present value of the future earnings that are expected to be generated from licensing these shows around the world for as long as people are interested in watching.

The broad accounting category of Goodwill and Other Intangible Assets shows $113 million. Most of this amount is associated with the acquisition of the CBS-affiliated television station WIVB in Buffalo. The assets include FCC licenses, a consulting agreement with the previous owner of the station, a noncompetition agreement with the previous owner, network affiliation rights, and other unidentified intangible assets of the station. Since the $113 million amount is derived form the recent transaction price, at which the property exchanged between unrelated parties, the amount can be considered as currently representative of market value, yet only 3% of the total revenues ($12 million) for 1989 were derived from the television station assets. In contrast, licensing rights are presented on the books at $7.3 million but contributed approximately $356 million of revenues. Clearly, something very important is very wrong.

The management of King World has not done anything to mislead investors. It has simply followed accepted accounting principles, and since its business is highly dependent on the development, ownership, and exploitation of intangible assets, its balance sheet is reduced to a useless mess.

King World is not alone. The same accounting system failures can be found on the balance sheets of Disney, Procter & Gamble, Dow Jones, Lotus Development Corp., Johnson & Johnson, and thousands of companies that have extraordinarily valuable intangible assets that were developed internally.

## The Marketplace Recognizes Intangible Value

A comparison of market value and book value for selected companies indicates that the investment community recognizes the value of intangible assets regardless of the lack of information that is provided in the accounting statements.

Expenditures that are made for land, factory buildings, office headquarters, truck fleets, and manufacturing equipment are all capitalized and presented as assets on the balance sheet. These assets meet all the requirements of the FASB definitions. Funds spent to acquire or build these assets become part of the equity of the company to the extent that their value exceeds liabilities. Stock prices typically include the value of these assets. A question arises, however, about the extent to which the market price of a stock reflects the intangible assets of trademarks and technology. Funds are expended to build trademarks through advertising. Other funds are used to create trade secrets and technology through research and development efforts. The expenditures are not capitalized but the assets are certainly quite real and meet all the required FASB definitions. The market, however, recognizes these assets and reflects their value in stock prices regardless of the failings of the accountant standards.

A ratio of the market price of a stock divided by the book value of the stock yields the market to book multiple, MK/BK ratio. If a company does not possess any intangible assets, then the price of a stock would very likely be close to the book value. The MK/BK ratio would equal approximately 1.0. As we have seen, the absence of intangible assets leaves a company capable of only generating a mediocre amount of earnings. Only a base rate of return on investment can be derived. Superior profits and growth prospects are unlikely and the value of the company tends toward the book value of equity. Utility companies are an excellent example.

The earnings of electric and gas utilities are regulated by governmental agencies. The companies are allowed to set prices for their services at a level that earns a fair rate of return on the assets that are used in the business. Intangible assets are not typically considered as a part of the rate base, so only the fixed asset investment can serve as the earnings power of the company. Utility stocks, as a result, tend to trade at a price that is approximately equal to the book value of the investment. A MK/BK ratio of 1.0 is typical.

When valuable technology, trademarks, or other intangible assets are present among unregulated businesses, they contribute to the earnings of the company far above the contribution of the fixed assets. Stock prices reflect this earnings power and trade above the book value of the stock, sometimes substantially.

A regression analysis of advertising expenditures was conducted to see if the market recognizes the long-term value of the trademarks that are being created and maintained by the advertising expenditures. The analysis used the market to book value ratio of selected companies versus the amounts spent on advertising to show that advertising expenditures are seen as asset-building investments that deserve recognition in the stock price. Exhibit 9-3 shows that as the amounts of advertising expenditures (shown as a percentage of

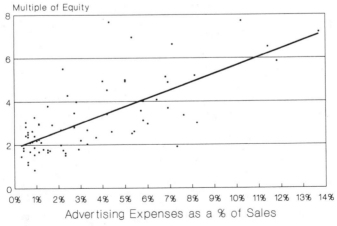

*Exhibit 9-3*   Market Multiples Related to Advertising Expenses

revenues for each company) increased, the price of the stock above book value also increased. The companies selected were taken from a list that annually appears in *Advertising Age* of companies that have spent the most amount of money on advertising. As spending increased, the ratio of the market to book value increased.

A lack of correlation would have indicated that the market did not recognize the value of the trademarks.

Another example of this trend using research and development expenditures confirms that the marketplace reflects the value of trade secrets and patented technology in stock prices. Exhibit 9-4 shows a regression analysis of R&D spending (as a percentage of revenues) for selected pharmaceutical companies with the MK/BK ratio for the same companies. As spending levels grow, the market rewards the company price with a higher market to book multiple; not because investors reward endless spending, but because valuable intangible assets are being created.

In the past, fundamental analysis taught that a stock price that was equal to or below the book value of a company represented the possibility of having identified a bargain investment. In the age of intangible assets, this simple indicator is no longer reliable. A company that is priced at a MK/BK ratio of 2.0 or higher can actually still be undervalued if the inherent value of the intangible assets is not

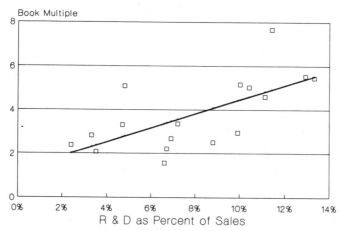

*Exhibit 9-4*    Market Multiples and R&D Spending for the Pharmaceutical Industry

fully appreciated. As discussed in Chapter 10, MK/BK ratios are no longer a useful screening device for finding undervalued stocks.

## International Complications

Analysis and comparison of U.S. companies with foreign companies are complicated by the inconsistencies of U.S. accounting practices. Accounting practices in different countries handle intangible assets in different ways. Japanese, German, and U.K. standards are very different. For example, in the United Kingdom, a company can place the value of intangible assets on its balance sheet at anytime. A triggering event, such as an acquisition, is not required to implement the strategy. Any fine morning, the CEO of a U.K. company can decide that intangible assets should be placed on the balance sheet. In the blink of an eye, intangible assets can be added. The effect on the balance sheet can be formidable.

Shareholders' equity doubled for Cadbury Schweppes during 1989 by 307 million pounds sterling and profits had little to do with it. The company decided to include the value of trademarks on the balance sheet. It owns the internationally recognized brand names of Canada Dry, Crush, Trebor, Bassetts, and Poulain. In another case, Britain's Ranks Hovis McDougall Plc, often called the Pillsbury of the United Kingdom, added 678 million pounds sterling ($1.2 billion) to the equity of the company by putting the value of 40 brands on its balance sheet.

The huge increases in the value of total assets not only increase equity but play havoc with balance sheet financial ratios. Before the introduction of brand names onto the balance sheet of Grand Metropolitan Plc, the debt of the company represented 50% of equity. After the brands were placed on the balance sheet, the debt ratio dropped to 14%. Grand Metropolitan added $1 billion to its balance sheet with the brand name value of Smirnoff vodka after it purchased Heublin. Then it went after Pillsbury. Some analysts think that Grand Metropolitan was able to finance the $5.7 billion Pillsbury purchase price because of the enhanced financial picture that the billion dollar Smirnoff value gave to the balance sheet. Martin Sorrell of WPP Group (parent company to the advertiser J. Walter Thompson and Hill & Knowlton) doesn't agree: "No bank is going to attribute value to intangible assets just because we've written them up."[13] Yet when WPP Group put the associated brand names of J. Walter Thompson and Hill & Knowlton onto the balance sheet its equity jumped by over $200 million. Sorrell explained why he valued the intangibles: "The balance sheet should give a true and fair view of value, and traditional accounting concepts don't do that for service companies."[14]

A U.S. company could actually possess identical financial conditions, asset bases, intangible asset values, and profitability prospects when compared to an identical U.K. company but comparison of the financial reports could unfortunately lead to the conclusion that the U.K. company was a superior investment. It would show more assets, higher equity, lower debt ratios, and higher profit margins.

In addition to the difficulty presented for comparative company analysis, it has been argued that British companies have an advantage in the amount that they can afford to pay for acquisitions in the United States. Our own accounting practices give advantages to foreign buyers.

## How to Find the Missing Information

Accounting statements have the mission of informing interested parties about the financial condition and profitability of a company. The mission is to present a fair and complete picture of the company. It must be clear by now that the current state of accounting practices in the United States is bungling the mission. Too many important facts about intangible assets are missing. Until the system is fixed, investors must work harder to independently research companies and their assets. The primary means to accomplish this are published research information from various sources.

Sources of published information that can help to fill the intangible asset information gap are described below. If intangible assets are particularly important to a company, these publications will

---

[13] Dana Wechsler, "Britain's Goodwill Games," *Forbes*, October 2, 1989, p. 65.
[14] See footnote 13.

identify and discuss the nature and characteristics of keystone intangibles.

## 10K Reports

A fabulous place to begin company research is the annual 10K Form that is filed with the Securities and Exchange Commission. Put the glossy annual report aside and read the 10K. Extraordinary details about the following topics are usually included:

Business description
Acquisition news
Sources of revenue
Marketing programs
Industry background
Competitor strengths
Government regulation
Employee count
List of operating centers
Overview of legal proceedings

From the perspective of intangible assets the 10K very often identifies and describes patents, trademarks, and copyrights that are important to ongoing operations. If license agreements with suppliers or customers are significantly important, the 10K will also cover these topics. Research and development programs are discussed for companies that are technologically oriented. Often the amounts spent on research and development are summarized. When trademarks are a vital business asset, advertising programs are reviewed and the amounts spent to support the marks are presented.

The narrative presentation of a 10K is well balanced. Favorable aspects of the business are focused on, with attention given to weaknesses. Discussion of management's plans for the future is often absent from 10Ks. The glossy annual report is the place to find the opinions and expectations of management.

Most companies are quite willing to send copies of 10Ks to any interested investor.

## Prospectuses

An old prospectus that was associated with a completed financing can still have, depending on its age, a comprehensive amount of information. Much of the same information that is required to be in the 10K is presented in prospectuses. In addition, more details about management plans and expectations are presented. Even though a prospectus is a selling document, there is good reason to give the information that is presented at least a minimum of credibility. Government regulations specify the areas to be covered. Incorrect and misleading disclosures are a criminal offense. As such, the information can be counted on to be fairly reliable.

## Trade Associations

It seems that if two or more people are in the same business a trade association is formed. Membership in these associations is comprised of industry participants. These organizations collect data about industry sales, costs, regulations, competitors, employees, and changing conditions. Many publish reports that are available to all interested parties. Staff members at trade associations are very helpful. They have a vast collection of contacts from within the industry and can recommend publications to read along with industry experts to interview for more insights. Identification of the appropriate trade association can quickly be accomplished at most reference libraries.

Many associations publish trade journals that cover industry conditions and events. Continued review of these publications allows investors to absorb the essence of the industry and develop a *feel* for events and conditions that make a difference to investment performance. Technical journals can be a good source of technological and patent information. Some of the articles may be written by key personnel that work at the company being studied.

## Brokerage Reports

Often prepared by security analysts who specialize in one or two industries, brokerage reports provide a detailed review of an industry and centrally compare the strengths and weaknesses of major industry participants. Also presented are the expectations of an investment expert who spent many years focusing research activities. Great insight can be gained from reading these reports but they must be read with caution. They are written to promote and sell securities. A more thorough cautioning about brokerage reports is presented in Chapter 10.

## Computer Clipping Services

Many inexpensive services allow subscribers to access a broad library of information. Clipping files can be created to collect articles of interest. Compuserv offers access to many news sources through a program called *Executive News Search*. By establishing a file of key words, investors can collect the most current news about technology, trademarks, licensing, joint ventures, infringement cases, advertising programs, and all other categories of intangible assets that exist. Time is saved because a huge assortment of reference publications can be screened simultaneously. Fees are limited to only those instances when articles that satisfy the parameters of the clipping file are met. Computerized investment research is one of the best methods for filling the intangible asset information gap.

## Company Information

Most companies are eager to assist investment research and quickly provide many of the following types of information to interested parties:

> Speeches by company personnel
> Court testimony by company executives
> Press releases
> Product literature
> Product manuals
> Annual meeting transcripts

A serious investigation should include reading all of the previously identified information from major competitors as well. The annual reports, 10Ks, prospectuses, and security analyst reports will view the subject company from different perspectives.

The best of all research worlds would have an accounting system that recognized the value of intangible assets and would consistently present them in financial statements. Until such an Eden is created, more grass roots research is needed and intangible asset information will need to be cobbled together from different sources.

# 10

# WATCH OUT FOR HIGH-TECH STORY STOCKS

Until now we have focused on the profit potential of proven innovations where intellectual property has successfully been commercialized by an established company. Successful products have been created and loyal customers have been cultivated. Market share has been captured and a history of excess profitability exists. This chapter discusses another form of intangible asset investment that is also available in the form of embryonic high-tech, high-risk ventures. Companies that have an idea and little else.

These companies are based on a vision, a dream, and hope. They are based on the most intangible asset of all— human imagination and ingenuity. Often these investments are referred to as *story stocks*, because the only highlights that can be presented as a reason to invest in them is a technological idea and a *story* about how the research might turn into a product that will make the world happier and investors much richer.

Story stocks usually possess a general theory involving the transformation of a technical hypothesis into a commercial business. Stories can involve:

Medicines to cure cancer
Metal alloys for cars that don't rust
Radar systems to find oil reserves
Private company space programs
Nuclear powered aircraft
Smokeless cigarettes

High technology isn't always a part of the story. In one case, the *story* was based on a clothing designer name that would be used for upscale wedding dresses to be exclusively distributed across the nation. The story explained that the well healed yuppie generation was marrying later, had refined tastes, and the money to live the dream. It sounded great. The story didn't include, however, that no one in the yuppie generation had ever heard of the supposedly great designer.

Great potential can be derived from investments in embryonic technology. The chance to become an initial stockholder of the next Microsoft Corporation, Apple Computer, Syntex, Federal Express, IBM, or Merck can overwhelm the common sense of even the most realistic investor. Embryonic technology presents the greatest opportunity for huge investment profits but it also possesses great potential for total loss.

Sometimes success creates entire new industries, as occurred when Apple Computer emerged from the garage. More often though the technical hypothesis doesn't make the transition from the lab to the factory. Or the investment entitles you to a share of excess wedding dress inventories.

Opportunities to invest in these most intangible investments are usually presented as initial public offerings of common stock (IPOs) or participation in venture capital partnerships.

Investors should expect to earn very high rates of return on story stocks because very high levels of investment risk are involved.

Story stocks usually *lack* most of the following characteristics of a going concern:

Sales prospects
Earnings history
Manufacturing assets
Developed products
Definition of market size

Winning stock selection is hard enough when the investment candidates have decades of track records. Story stocks require imagination and luck.

A favorite pastime on Wall Street is to estimate the total market for the end product of a new story stock. Without fail, the total size that is presented in the prospectus is in the billion dollar range . . . *and if Brand New Company, Inc. can capture only 10% of the market it will be a $100 million company.* The imagination immediately focuses on the grand possibilities and ignores that Brand New Company, Inc. doesn't have a commercially viable technology, sales force, manufacturing plant, federally approved product, or even any cash in the bank. Money in the bank is the purpose of the invitation to invest. Also forgotten is consideration for the current activities of the competition. You can bet that they aren't just sitting around.

## A Risky Record

Venture capital investment in a story stock is risky. When the possibility of total investment loss is strong, the potential for return should be high. One survey that was published by Venture Economics, Inc. of Wellesley, Massachusetts, covered over 200 companies that were venture capital story stocks. The results presented in Exhibit 10-1 demonstrate the risks involved:

Poor investment results occurred 70% of the time. *Losers* denote ventures that did not work out as expected and were liquidated. *Living dead* is an endearing term applied to ventures that have not performed as expected and are not expected to achieve the originally planned happy ending. They continue on only because no one has pulled the plug. The remaining 30% show different levels of success

*Exhibit 10-1*    Venture Capital Investments: How the Story Ended

| Percentage of Total | Status | Return on Initial Investment |
| --- | --- | --- |
| 40% | Losers | Total loss |
| 30% | Living dead | Total loss |
| 20% | Not bad | Two to five times |
| 8% | Good deal | Five to ten times |
| 2% | Wow | Ten times plus |

but only 2% achieved extraordinary levels of return. Remember, the losers and living dead involved a total loss of the initial investment.

## Paradise Lost

Embryonic technology ventures combine the unbridled enthusiasm of creative dreamers with the profit driven motivations of stock-brokers. Without meaning to, and sometimes with malice of forethought, a whirl of excitement is created for a specific research idea or even entirely new industries such as biotechnology. Some of the great visions actually come to pass. Too many others just run through research money until someone compassionately puts the project out of everyone's misery. A few examples of great dreams that did not come true include the following:

  o *Nuclear jets.* During the late 1950s, the U.S. government spent millions of dollars on the development of nuclear powered aircraft. A prototype was built and tested. Just imagine the potential for deployment of such an aircraft. Fueling requirements could allow the aircraft to stay airborne, and ready for attack, for almost limitless amounts of time. Commercial aircraft applications could also ease much of the traveling delays associated with refueling and extend the range of jet travel beyond the wildest dreams of the time. Unfortunately, the nuclear aircraft engines were never able to produce enough thrust for lift-off.

  o *Shale oil.* Extraction of oil from shale rock was the technological achievement of the 1970s that would save us from the tyranny of the OPEC nations. Workable technology was developed and investments based on implementation were prepared by several companies. Suddenly, oil prices declined steeply as the tightly knit OPEC group began to unravel. Reduced oil prices made the shale oil technology economically obsolete. Only when oil was dearly priced was the new technology commercially viable. Economic conditions quickly changed the prospects for shale oil technology investments. Someday this technology may well be valuable intellectual property: depending of course on the future level of oil prices. Until then, an investment in this research project has provided little return.

○ *Synthetic leather.* Corfam ™ was a synthetic leather that DuPont developed at the cost of tens of million of dollars. All forms of leather products including shoes, briefcases, and handbags were expected to be greatly enhanced by the near indestructible material. The product was a flop because consumers didn't want to wear "plastic." Market perceptions were so powerful that the new invention, which met the performance requirements set for it, ultimately failed.

○ *Smokeless cigarettes.* A revolutionary cigarette was developed at an estimated cost to RJR Nabisco of $300 million only to be pulled from the market after only 5 months of limited consumer testing. The cigarette eliminated side-stream smoke that nonsmokers find objectionable. Smokers could feed their habit without infringing on the rights of nonsmokers. Expectations at RJR were sky-high. Unfortunately, the technology required smokers to use an unfamiliar aluminum inhaler, ignite the product with only high quality butane lighters, and study a four page instruction booklet that accompanied each pack. The new product complicated the once simple act of lighting-up, making the new product into a cigarette that even avid smokers did not want. It also made the smokeless cigarette into the most disastrous new product introduction in decades.

## Bad Things Can Happen to Good Investors

Some of the things that can happen to exciting innovation investments involve the following:

1. Markets that aren't ready for dramatic changes.
2. Government regulations that are not prepared.
3. Cost and benefit analyses that were too optimistic.
4. Development of superior competing technologies.
5. Inability to establish distribution channels.
6. Failed transitions from pilot plant operations to fullscale manufacturing.

Technology does not always work as expected. As research is begun, complications are likely to be uncovered and cause delays. Delays can pile up and research funds are burned faster than originally expected. If research proceeds without interruption, the transition from pilot plants (small-scale production levels in a tightly controlled environment) to mass production may introduce obstacles that were not expected, causing an overrun of development budgets. Of course, the ultimate development catastrophe might determine that the technology just doesn't work—as happened with nuclear powered aircraft engines.

Even if the technology is proved and can make the transition beyond the pilot plant to commercial production levels, the question about market demand still remains. Will the market accept the new technology? Old habits are not given up easily. Fax machines have been available for almost 20 years but only just recently have they come into wide use. Expensive high-tech products aren't exactly impulse items that sell after a 15 minute sales presentation. The final cost of the new product can be many times the price tag of the item. Conversion to a new high-tech system can involve construction of special facilities for the new equipment and can require advanced training for the staff who will be responsible for operating and maintaining the new system. When the price tag is big, buyers most often must run the decision through several management levels for approval. The lag time between sales contact and final purchase decision can run for a year, depending on the product and the price tag. Companies that are small, young, and cash poor can get killed when they are dependent on a new product that involves a long sales lag. This can occur even when the new product is the best mousetrap in town. If the market isn't ready for change, investments in the best technological breakthrough can go unrewarded.

Some companies are sensitive to the slow machinery of government approvals. Technological advances can easily push far ahead of the government procedures for approval, as experienced in the biotechnology field.

Start-ups are risky. They are lacking in all areas including an operating history of revenues and earnings. They lack products and sometimes even basic research and development have not been completed. Risks are also presented by government regulations, identification of actual market size, and achievable market penetration. And don't expect competitors to just sit around.

## Selling High-Tech Story Stocks

Story stock salespeople are not necessarily evil. They want to believe. They are selling hope: hope that you will be investing in the next IBM; hope that the new technology will bring a sort of alchemy to everything that it touches. Hope sells.

A stockbroker interrupts your day with a telephone call that begins: "Would you like to make a killing in a new company that is about to go public?" Even the most jaded investor is hard pressed to hang up. It doesn't seem that there is any harm in just listening. Then the stockbroker launches into a well rehearsed presentation highlighting the *unlimited* potential for great profits: a sales pitch that is designed to peak interest and move the goods. As the pitch continues, it is best to remember that stockbroker means *salesperson*. Stockbrokers use many titles, which are all designed to convey an impression of expertise and accomplishment: account executive, financial planner, investment adviser, and financial consultant. Beware: they are salespeople; someone who is employed to sell products or services. For many, too many, of these salespeople the current stock that they are pushing is just another product on which commissions can be earned. Your investment nest egg is just another place to dump some of their inventory.

Commission dollars represent house payments, food, clothes, and personal gratification to stockbrokers just like everyone else who works for a living. They must sell in order to live the good life.

Adding to these pressures are quotas established by their employers. Further pressure to sell certain stocks comes from commission structures, designed to pay higher amounts of commission on certain investments.

Rounding out the pressure on your stockbroker is the pressure on the brokerage firm that acts as a market maker in certain stocks. They may have a lot of the stock in inventory and a great incentive to move it into your portfolio and out of theirs. Obscure stocks in which the company has a large inventory position heavily weight the investments of the brokerage firm in the particular stock. Commissions paid to the salespeople encourage them to move these goods. They can make significantly higher commissions on these obscure stocks than if they sell you IBM.

Getting into the field of investment sales requires a license. An 8 hour examination that tests understanding of financial terms and securities law must be passed to earn a license. The test does not cover investment theory, financial analysis capabilities, economic knowledge, accounting theory, business finance, or an understanding of stock market volatility. It does not test knowledge of any of the important aspects of successful companies—just cursory securities law. English majors, chemists, football players, and piano players can all take the test, pass, and begin selling investments in which they have a complete lack of fundamental training.

When high-tech intangible assets are the foundation of the story, the educational gap of your stockbroker is even more dangerous: for you, not your stockbroker. It is vital that sole reliance on the information provided by your broker be avoided. For the most part, it is a prepackaged and limited presentation. In all fairness, expecting your stockbroker to understand biotechnology, nuclear physics, optic fiber communications, or even microwave kitchen products is a little unreasonable. Consider the comments of Nobel laureate Sir Peter Medawar: "Biologists work very close to the frontier between bewilderment and understanding." When stockbrokers begin to hustle investments that they barely understand, a disaster is close at hand.

Time to fill the educational gap just doesn't exist. Very often, a broker has more than a hundred customers to maintain and a large list of recommended stocks to push. All day is spent on the telephone selling. If quotas are not satisfied by selling to a broker's existing customer list, then countless telephone calls to prospects—potential customers—are made in marathon telephone sessions. Quotas must be met and telephone calls are the method.

Sometimes the pressure forces a few to become extremely pushy. They start with persuasive phrases.

"This situation is going to be a home run."
"The market doesn't understand the intrinsic value of the technology involved."
"In just a little while this stock is going to pop."

If you still hesitate, then abuse can quickly enter the conversation.

"Do you want to always be on the sidelines?"
"Its time to play in the big league."
"Only a loser would pass this one by."

Stock analysis is not the province of your stockbroker.

## Brokers' Research Departments

Research departments are the source of investment ideas. Security analysts are employed to provide ideas and background research that supports the recommendations. Emphasis is placed on finding reasons to buy stocks.

Analysts attend industry seminars, read trade journals, study annual reports, interview company executives, and crunch numbers. They must decipher information from many sources and look at the plans and expectations of company managers with skepticism. In their search for reality, they must separate into neat piles reality, blind enthusiasm, distortions, and outright lies.

Besides the pressure to cover many different company stocks, there are other conflicting pressures. Glowing reports are far more useful than gloom and doom pronouncements. Brokerage firm stockbrokers want upbeat reports that can be used as a selling tool. Brokerage firms want to impress potential investment banking clients with great coverage of the potential customer's company. The analysts themselves have an inherent bias toward writing reports that help sell stocks. It centers on a desire to distinguish themselves as researchers who can find winners.

Unfortunately, when eminent scientists are in fundamental disagreement regarding research strategies and the possibility for commercially viable products, how can the humble security analyst find reality and make the correct call?

Conflict of interests round out the pressure on analysts. Primary information sources for them are the managers of the companies that they follow. Industry insights, capital budgets, new product plans, earnings forecasts, and estimates of market size can all be obtained or confirmed by company managers. Most of the time the managers are eager to provide analysts with access to this information and with access to key personnel within the company. An unfaltering report, however, can quickly erode relationships, with the company leaving the analyst out of the information loop. Flattering reports can keep the channels of information open but may be undeserved. If you think that some research reports are slanted, good for you. You're correct.

The ultimate pressure on security analysts was unilaterally provided last year when a well known security analyst at Janney Montgomery was fired for making unauthorized comments to the press about the prospects for the gaming industry in Atlantic City. Donald Trump threatened the brokerage with legal action if the analyst was not fired. Citing unauthorized comments to the press, the brokerage firm bowed to the pressure of a financial powerhouse and fired a veteran analyst for reporting his opinion—fired for doing his job. The *Washington Post* on March 27, 1990 asked: "If Donald Trump can force your stockbroker to fire its top expert on casino stocks because the analyst predicted publicly that Trump's newest gaming palace may fail, then how can you believe what your broker tells you about Trump casino shares, or anything else?" The unvarnished truth is only popular on Wall Street when it is good. Otherwise, your broker may have to lie to keep his or her job.

## Story Stocks Run Like Fashion Fads

Fads on Wall Street are as common as color changes on Madison Avenue. Biotechnology was the magic solution to all problems in the early 1980s. When Genentech went public in 1980, the stock was offered at $35 per share. In 20 minutes the price rose to $89. This success opened the floodgates. For the rest of the decade biotechnology companies, with great stories and without, hit the market at unbelievable offering prices: all promising to find the magic bullet that would cure cancer, AIDS, birth defects, and hair loss. Actual benefits are only just now starting to emerge, while many of the initial investments in these companies have long ago been lost. Reality has finally struck Wall Street. Biotechnology stock prices are more likely to reflect the long time lag between start-up and profits. A lot of money was lost in learning this lesson.

On the horizon, the investment fad for the 1990s is likely to be *green* stocks: anything and everything that promise to protect and clean our fragile ecological environment. The boom has already started, where specialized mutual funds are being established to invest in these companies. The fad that sells intangible asset stocks today says: "Investing in my stock will save the environment and make you rich, all at the same time."

Green stock mutual funds are beginning to grow like organically fed weeds. Fidelity Investments, Merrill Lynch, and John Hancock all have funds that focus on companies that can help clean the environment, or which at least won't hurt the ecology further. Fidelity described the fund as "a direct play on the fastest growth industry of the 1990s." The green stock fad is spreading faster than the *Valdez* oil spill. In addition to mutual funds, greenies include foundations, public pensions, private pensions, universities, labor unions, churches, insurance companies, and banks. As demand for these stocks rises, the valuations of these companies will become unrealistic. High-risk story stocks promising to save the Earth from the excesses of the human race will fill the draws of stockbrokers and the calls for your investment dollars will come. Sales presentations will focus on advisor boards, eminent consultants, glowing forecasts, and untested technology. Absent again from the analysis will be an outline of viable products, an earnings history, sales prospects, and a description of corporate assets.

Special care is needed when fads start to run away. When investments are being priced at levels that reject all the old standards of value, look closer. Then look again.

## Take Control

We fall victim to magic bullet sales talk because our nation and way of life were founded on contrary ideas, big dreams, grand hopes, and the chance to escape oppression and reinvent Eden. The glory of the United States is the great progress that has been made toward this grand dream. Everything still seems possible. When a crazy promise comes from the *experts* on Wall Street, we want to believe the story.

Common sense and unemotional thinking can save you from high-tech stories. If you don't believe that the projections make sense, trust your skepticism. Ask questions and do research. More people have gotten into trouble by saying to themselves: "I guess *they* know what they are doing." In most cases, they do. . . taking your money and gambling with it.

Peter Lynch, legendary manager of the Fidelity Magellan Fund, regularly ponders the question about why investors spend countless hours researching their next purchase of a television set while readily plunking down $10,000 or $20,000 on a stock that they don't know anything about and whose business they do not understand.

---

Key Investment Concept #28

Never give into the pressure to buy now! Ask for research reports and read them. Then investigate the company further on your own. Ask questions that are based on common sense.

---

The successful companies that have been discussed have established records, strong market positions, and proven products. Investing in intangible corporate America does not mean that candidates for investment dollars should be limited to the cutting edge of technology. A lot of money has been made in dull businesses that possess valuable intangible assets. As we've discussed, some of the most valuable intangible assets possessed aren't related in any way with technological breakthroughs.

---

**Key Investment Concept #29**

Successfully investing in companies with intangible assets does not necessarily require gambling in high-tech, high-risk ventures.

---

## Speculative Safeguards

When the urge to make an embryonic intangible asset investment is overwhelming, the following rules can limit the down-side possibilities.

**1.** *Prepare to be patient* and to have your patience tested. Embryonic intangible asset investments do not generally yield profits for several years, let alone the next quarter. The investment should not be watched for stock market movements, blips upward, or dips downward. Nervous investors are usually very uncomfortable with this type of speculation. Self-assessment of investment psychology may be a prudent first step when approaching this type of speculation.

**2.** *Allocate funds that you can afford to lose* to these speculative investments. Money that is needed for the house payment next month should never be invested in such ventures. Similarly, funds that have been set aside for college education or retirement are better invested elsewhere.

**3.** *Limit losses by reevaluating the entire venture* if more funding is requested. Embryonic technology can provide surprises as development occurs. Basic research may turn up more areas that require investigation. Government regulators may want more testing. Production quality may require higher levels of volume through-put. More money will be needed if any of these events occur. Reevaluate the entire investment if more funds are requested. Check if the market still exists and look to see if competitors have passed by the technology that is still in development. A reevaluation may indicate that it is better to accept the loss of the original investment. When the truth is unpleasant, it should be accepted just as quickly as when it is encouraging. Don't throw more money into the venture until the reasons for the delay are completely spelled out and only if a reevaluation of the strategy still makes sense.

**4.** *Be a contrary thinker.* Embryonic and revolutionary ideas tend to run against established thinking. If the venture made complete sense to everyone, then risk capital probably would not have been sought in the first place. The entrepreneur in whom you are investing might never have ventured out of the corporate office to attempt the new project. Established wisdom would have provided corporate approval and funding. Naysayers may attempt to make the investment seem like an oddball. If your initial research is encouraging, then stand by it.

**5.** *Focus speculative investments on ventures that are involved in areas that you understand.* This is especially true for high-tech research projects. You will have a much better understanding of the true possibilities and the real risk involved. It is possible also that you can contribute information and insights that will help things along.

**6.** *Diversify* the funds that are committed to these most intangible asset investments. Failure rates are high when the business involves turning dreams into products. Betting all the money on one dream can turn into a nightmare.

## Final Analysis

Some of the greatest inventions in the world have been created by dreamers who were funded by visionaries. The United States would not possess the quality of life that we enjoy without these risk takers. Investing in dreams, however, is risky. We tend to remember the successes of Edison, Ford, Rockefeller, Gates, and others who have won their bets. It is vital to remember that as you approach the intangible asset investment of dreams that a lot of money has been lost by too many people who did not ask questions and did not understand the risks. The venture capital study previously mentioned showed that money was lost 70% of the time. This happened to sophisticated venture capitalists who had a full understanding of the business and the risks.

Remember that the final decision is your responsibility. Security analysts can conduct research and brokers can call it to your attention. Ideas can be presented and compelling viewpoints can be pressed. But remember that these advisers have conflicting pressures where their self-interests are more likely to win out over your interests. In the area of intangible assets, the opportunity for confusion multiplies. Regardless of all the security laws that exist and all the remedies established by our legal system, the fundamental principle for intangible asset investments is still, *Let the Buyer Beware.*

---

Key Investment Concept #30

Spend more time researching your next investment than you spent deciding on your last television purchase.

---

# 11

# TEN OF THE BEST

This chapter provides a review of the key intangible asset characteristics that propel earnings and drive winning stock performance. At the end of the chapter, ten companies, considered to be among the best intangible asset investments currently available, are presented.

This chapter is not intended to replace vitally important fundamental analysis. Excellent reference books on fundamental analysis are listed at the end of this chapter. They expertly outline the important aspects of conducting comprehensive fundamental analysis. This chapter aims at highlighting important considerations that are unfortunately and rarely stressed but that deserve more complete investigation. Only when the concepts that have been presented in this book are coupled with the traditional investigation techniques of fundamental analysis will investors be ready to buy and sell stocks in the 1990s and beyond.

## After the Fundamentals Are Studied

Fundamental analysis looks for companies that have strong and stable earnings growth, low debt, competitive barriers to competition, and low stock prices in relation to the other companies. When traditional fundamental analysis is complete, then intangible asset analysis must begin. Intangible assets are present when some or all of the following characteristics are present:

1.  Above-average profit margins.
2.  Stable profits.
3.  High amounts of advertising expenditures a percentage of sales.
4.  Consistent advertising.
5.  High amounts of research and development expenditures as a percentage of sales.
6.  Consistent research and development.
7.  High market to book ratios.
8.  High levels of debt ratios when compared to total assets.
9.  Expanding exploitation announcements.
10. High amounts of sales for each dollar invested in working capital and fixed assets.
11. High levels of gross profit.
12. High levels of operating income.
13. High returns on working capital and fixed assets.
14. High PE ratio valuations.
15. Joint ventures.
16. License agreements.

Above-average profit margins usually are derived from two broad areas as previously discussed. The first can be premium selling prices, where the majority of the premium can be brought to the bottom line as profitability. Trademarks have been shown to fall within this category. The second can be production cost savings that are achieved by use of other valuable intangible assets like patented process technology.

The profitability advantage may be at the gross profit level where manufacturing costs are optimized. However, it is quite possible that the gross profit margin for a superior intangible asset company is little better then the average competitor. The superior earnings performance might then be derived from optimization of operating costs such as selling, administration, distribution, or the reduction of overhead costs.

The ability to sustain above-average profits is vital when assessing stocks. Trademarks can be tarnished and the advantages of patents are limited by a set clock. Acceptance of above-average profits as being a continuous phenomenon is dangerous unless the intangible assets that are responsible for the earnings are studied and understood.

Whenever a trademark is the key intangible asset, close scrutiny should be given to the amount spent on advertising. A review of the most recent years, going back at least 5 years, should be made to see that advertising is maintained. As we have seen, stock performance can directly be related to the maintenance of well known trademarks. As such, when investigating a company that depends on trademarks it is important to be assured that a consistent level of advertising is being maintained. It is very important to watch for announcements where management has decided to temporarily cutback advertising expenses. Very often this technique is used to curtail short-term earnings depressions but can quickly backfire into a long-term deterioration of earnings. The temptation to curtail advertising expenses is often greatest when the advertising exposure is needed most. During recessions it is even more important to watch for shortsighted cut-back announcements. Trademarks are fragile and require continued advertising. When strong advertising support is detected, investment success is more likely. When cut-backs are announced, stock holdings should be reconsidered.

The same technique of investigating expense trends is important for research and development efforts. If the intangible assets of the company being considered for investment are of a technological nature, attention should be focused on the research budget. Historical reviews of the amount spent on research and development should be conducted to detect the consistency and hopefully growing commitment to research and development. As with advertising, when an announcement is made by management that temporary research cut-backs are planned, investors should see this as a signal to possibly sell the stock or at least reevaluate desirability of the investment position. Whenever possible, an analysis of new product introductions should be conducted. The transformation of inventions into commercial products is an area where U.S. companies have lagged behind. Companies that consistently make the transition from laboratory benchtop to retail outlets are superior companies. These are the places to put investment funds.

When assessing the valuation by the market of intangible asset stocks, a high ratio of the market price to the accounting book value should not be considered overvaluation. Since many intangible assets are not represented on balance sheets, the book values of these companies are very often grossly understated. When the market price captures some or all of the value of the intangible assets, a market to book ratio of extraordinarily high multiples can result. This does not necessarily mean that the stock is grossly overvalued—only that the market has recognized the value of some of the intangible assets. Historically, many great investors have focused on a market to book ratio of 1.0 or less as an indication that a stock is being neglected or undervalued. With the growing importance of intangible assets, and dominance of them in many corporations, this old rule is extremely unreliable. Today a company could be trading at two, three, or more times its book value and still be undervalued.

High debt ratios should also not be looked on as an indication of a poor investment characteristic. Certainly a company that has a huge amount of debt should be studied carefully to assure that the debt obligations can be met. However, focusing on a ratio of long-term debt to total assets will no longer provide a clear indication of the credit worthiness. The key assets of many companies are simply not presented on the balance sheet but sophisticated lending institutions are recognizing the value of intangible assets and allowing companies to have high debt to asset ratios. If the values of intangible assets were included on balance sheets, the high ratios would be adjusted and could easily fall into line with industry averages. Since intangible assets are not shown on the balance sheet, debt ratios may wrongly indicate an overleveraged position. A much more useful test of debt capacity is to look at the ratio of "times-interest-earned." This ratio looks at the number of times that the interest expense can be met by the operating income of the company. When the operating income can cover interest expenses at an amount that is several times that of the interest expense, the debt levels are satisfactory despite the indications that are presented by the debt to asset ratios.

In each industry a certain amount of investment is needed to generate each dollar of sales. Intangible assets quite often take the place of fixed asset investments, reducing the need to maintain larger amounts of net working capital and capital equipment. In those instances, a very high sales to fixed assets and net working capital investment ratio will result.

Companies that possess valuable intangible assets are more likely to show a high return on investments (ROI). This ratio is simply calculated by dividing net income by the summation of shareholders' equity and long-term debt (invested capital). When using the book value of invested capital, a high ratio of ROI is usually the result of having significant intangible assets that are not measured on the balance sheet.

Many companies that have valuable intangible assets will also have very high stock prices in relation to earnings (high PE multiples). Historically, investors have passed by companies with high PE ratios as being overvalued. Another reason though for a high PE ratio is that the profits of intangible asset companies can be very badly understated. Research and development budgets as well as advertising expenses should more correctly be looked on as capital expenditures that build and maintain important intangible assets. When plant and equipment are purchased or created, the amount spent is capitalized on the balance sheet and not charged to the income statement as expenses. Near-term profits are therefore unaffected by the capital expenditures except to the extent that appropriate depreciation charges are allocated to current activities. When research expenditures and advertising budgets are charged as current expenses, however, the long-term assets created are not being properly capitalized as long-term assets. As a result, the earnings of intangible asset companies are understated. High PE ratios are the result but do not necessarily indicate that the company is overvalued. Investors wishing to adjust for this problem should recompute the net income of the company after adding back the research and development budgets and advertising expenses. These items of expense are then treated as capital expenditures and not charged against current earnings. When the adjusted earnings are related to the price of the shares, lower PE ratios are the result.

## Expanding Exploitation

The most important part of intangible asset analysis centers on identifying exploitation strategies. Winning stocks in the future will be those of company's that:

1.  Use their intangible assets for internal expansion.
2.  Obtain licenses to use the intangible assets of others.
3.  Grant licenses of intangible assets for use by others in exchange for royalty income.
4.  Contribute intangible assets to joint venture partnerships.

Monitoring these activities can also help to identify future acquisition candidates. Holding the stock of a company that is about to be acquired has traditionally been lucrative. In many instances, larger companies are buying technology, funding research, or entering joint ventures with smaller companies. The smaller company then represents a future acquisition target. If nothing else, the investment by the larger company is affirmation of the potential associated with the smaller company. Long before anyone had heard of Genentech, Eli Lilly was buying technology from the company for use in producing a human form of insulin. Eli Lilly never acquired Genentech, but had anyone noticed the activities of Eli Lilly and pursued an investment in Genentech the rewards were astounding.

## Ten of the Best.

The rest of this chapter presents a brief overview of ten companies that are considered to be among the best intangible asset managers currently available for investment. Conditions may change between the time this final chapter is written and the book hits the street, but most likely these excellent intangible asset companies will still be excellent.

## The Walt Disney Company

Disney is an entertainment company that was founded on perennial intangible assets. Mickey Mouse, Donald Duck, and the gang helped rear a generation or two. With business interests in theme parks, film production, retail products, children's books, and educational toys, this company is one of the best intangible asset exploiters in the world.

At first the company profited from animated motion picture films, which filled a library with classics like *Cinderella, Snow White, Pinocchio,* and *Lady and the Tramp.* The same characters have been the basis of comic books and children's toys since the 1930s. This success has lead to the recent establishment by the company of three new book divisions.

The film successes of the company in animation led to the creation of Touchstone Pictures, which produces quality films like Good Morning Vietnam, The Good Mother, Beaches, Who Framed Roger Rabbit, and Three Men and a Baby.

The first theme park, Disneyland, was located in Anaheim, California. Its huge success fostered the establishment of an East Coast version of the park in Orlando, Florida—Disney World. Not satisfied with domestic success, the company built a Disneyland in Japan and is planning to open EuroDisneyland just outside Paris in 1992.

The retail products of the company use the characters that are seen by hundreds of millions of people each year at theaters, at theme parks, and on television.

In retailing, every conceivable product that can be trademarked has Disney characters, including wristwatches, T-shirts, hats, and stuffed dolls. This has led to the establishment of over 20 upscale retail outlets that sell only Disney products.

Recently, the company tried to purchase the Muppets from Henson Associates to give itself more perennial characters to carry on the magic of this company.

Disney is a one-of-kind enterprise that is certainly impossible to duplicate.

*Disney Highlights*

Recent sales: $4.6 billion
Average sales growth 1980–1989: 19.6%
Recent net income: $703 million
Average net income growth 1980–1989: 20.1%
Net income profit margin, 5 year average: 12.5%
Recent long-term debt as percentage of capital: 19.2%
Recent return on equity: 25.9%

Disney has high growth in sales and income, stable profits, low debt, and strong returns on investment. The company has a library of perennial intangible assets and knows how to exploit them.

A 10 year investment in the stock of Disney rewarded investors with a 24.6% rate of return.

## H. J. Heinz Company

Heinz is the leading producer of ketchup with over 50% of the U.S. market. The Heinz name is also placed on sauces, baby food, beans, vinegar, and pickles. A worldwide producer of food products, the company has a stable of well known trademarks, including Ore-Ida, 9-Lives, Chico-San, Orlando, Olivine, Plasion, Sperlari, Gulso, and Weight Watchers. The company enjoys the number 1 brand position in over 50% of its products. Through a combination of volume growth and cost cutting, the company has increased its operating profit margin every year since 1977, a feat seldom matched by any company, let alone a company that competes in the mature food sector.

In addition to a portfolio of well known trademarks, the company has a worldwide distribution network. It recently exploited this intangible asset further by acquiring Weight Watchers International, placing the diet food offerings of the company in grocery stores across the country. Improvements and additions to the Weight Watchers food offerings along with an advertising campaign that features Lynn Redgrave have greatly expanded the sales of the company.

*Heinz Highlights*

Recent sales: $5.8 billion
Average sales growth 1980–1989: 7.9%
Recent net income: $440 million
Average net income growth 1980–1989: 13.3%
Net income profit margin, 5 year average: 7.2%
Recent long-term debt as percentage of capital: 25.2%
Recent return on equity: 26.0%

Heinz displays steady sales growth in a mature market and continues to expand an already high net profit margin in a low-profit industry. The company has shown that it can exploit its famous trademark and has also extended the use of its distribution network through the acquisition of Weight Watchers.

A 10 year investment in the stock of Heinz rewarded investors with a 27.8% rate of return.

## Johnson & Johnson

In 1886 two brothers developed a dry sterilization process for the production of surgical dressings that were wrapped and sealed in separate packages and ready for immediate use. Innovative process technology and packaging are still the driving force behind J&J, which has expanded into one of the broadest product line companies in the health care industry. Product categories include consumer goods, ethical drugs, over-the-counter pharmaceuticals, medical instrumentals, surgical supplies, and dental products.

The continued focus on research is exemplified by the growing R&D budget, which reached $719 million by the end of 1989. The company's Jansen Research Group is well regarded for efficient commercialization of new discoveries. Jansen commercializes a new product for every 1000 compounds that it synthesizes, which is four times the industry rate. Unlike other companies that are dependent on the sales of one or two blockbuster products, J&J has 16 drugs with sales in excess of $50 million and another 7 drugs with sales over $100 million.

Product introductions in recent years include:

- HISMANAL antihistamine
- ACUVUE contact lenses
- EPREX, used by dialysis patients suffering from anemia
- The first diagnostic test for hepatitis C
- PREPULSID, a digestive treatment for chronic gastritis
- INTERCEED, a new product that prevents surgical adhesions
- IMODIUM, a new nonprescriptive antidiarrheal product

One of the best examples of joint ventures with extraordinary potential is the combination between J&J and Merck. The companies have formed Johnson & Johnson–Merck Consumer Pharmaceuticals Company to develop and market nonprescriptive medicines in the United States. J&J has a 50% stake in the joint venture, for which it has contributed its over-the-counter marketing expertise, along with its sales and distribution network. Merck brings to the party new product candidates and research capabilities that are the envy of the world. The joint venture has enjoyed a rapid start by acquiring over-the-counter drugs from ICI Americas, Inc., including the Mylanta line of antacid products and the Mylicon line of anti-gas products.

*Johnson & Johnson Highlights*

Recent sales: $9.8 billion
Average sales growth 1980–1989: 8.1%
Recent net income: $1.1 billion
Average net income growth 1980–1989: 11.7%
Net income profit margin, 3 year average: 10.8%
Recent long-term debt as percentage of capital: 22.0%
Recent return on equity: 28.3%

The "No More Tears" people are a research juggernaut that has a very broad product line and unparalleled intangible assets in the form of distribution networks, marketing expertise, and a new products research orientation. On top of it all, the new joint venture with Merck combines the best strengths of two of the best companies in the world.

A 10 year investment in the stock of Johnson & Johnson rewarded investors with a 20.0% rate of return.

## Loctite Corporation

Loctite manufactures engineering adhesives, sealants, specialty chemicals, coatings, and electroluminescent lighting systems. The products of the company are high-performance items used in medical products, electronics manufacturing, automotive maintenance, and other industrial applications. Specific products include thread locking adhesives, instant adhesives, structural adhesives, gasketing compounds, automobile body repair materials, electronics component sealants, lubricating compounds, and cleaning compounds.

The chief products of the company are anaerobic adhesives and sealants that have the characteristic of remaining in a liquid state while exposed to air and then hardening when introduced into an airless environment. Cyanoacrylate products of the company characteristically harden quickly when exposed to moisture.

Loctite's primary and most substantial intangible asset is the technological expertise that allows the company to develop custom adhesives and sealants for special customer purposes. The company maintains an active research effort, which is expected to introduce new products for fast curing adhesives, materials to bond plastic, and specialty silicones.

*Loctite Highlights*

Recent sales: $456 million
Average sales growth 1980–1989: 9.7%
Recent net income: $54.5 million
Average net income growth 1980–1989: 8.6%
Net income profit margin, 5 year average: 9.8%
Recent long-term debt as percentage of capital: 13.8%
Recent return on equity: 25.0%

Loctite has low debt, steady earnings growth, and the ability to deliver new products on a market-driven basis.

A 10 year investment in the stock of Loctite Corporation rewarded investors with only a 13.8% rate of return, but over the last 5 years investors have received a 29.8% rate of return from holding this stock.

## Merck & Company

Merck is the world's largest ethical drug manufacturer. Products are manufactured for both human and animal uses. The emphasis at Merck is on innovative research. Before 1990 is over, the company will spend $855 million on R&D: an increase of 14% over the amount spent in 1989. For the 10 years 1980 through 1989, the company has spent $4.5 billion on research. One of the new product introductions with great potential is PROSCAR, a drug used to reduce the size of enlarged prostates. Inflamed prostates are experienced by a huge percentage of older males. As the demographics of our population ages, this product will be a winner.

Strategic alliances provide a special opportunity for enhanced value with Merck. In addition to the joint venture with Johnson & Johnson that was previously covered (see Johnson & Johnson), Merck has entered into a research and marketing collaboration with DuPont. The focus is on the discovery of a class of novel therapeutic agents that promise to be the next generation of prescription medicines for treating high blood pressure and heart disease. A joint venture with DuPont is also planned where DuPont will contribute its entire pharmaceutical business and Merck will provide R&D expertise, foreign sales rights for a collection of established products, and developmental funds.

Merck was named by *Fortune* magazine as the most admired company for the fourth year in a row. *Business Week* magazine named the company one of the most innovative and *The Wall Street Journal* called Merck among the "select few companies poised to lead business into the 1990s." Exploitation of intangible assets through joint ventures and research expertise make this company one of the best intangible asset managers in the world.

*Merck Highlights*

Recent sales: $6.5 billion
Average sales growth 1980–1989: 10.2%
Recent net income: $1.5 billion
Average net income growth 1980–1989: 15.3%
Net income profit margin, 5 year average: 18.5%
Recent long-term debt as percentage of capital: 2.6%
Recent return on equity: 47.0%

A 10 year investment in the stock of Merck & Company rewarded investors with a 23.5% rate of return and over the last 5 years investors have received a 37.0% rate of return from holding this stock.

## Microsoft Corporation

Microsoft developed a broad line of systems software and applications software for microcomputers. The systems software of the company includes the MS-DOS operating system, which is the most widely used system for IBM PC and compatible computers. In addition, the MS-OS/2 operating system has been introduced for use with computers that are based on the Intel 80286 and 80386 microprocessor. Recently, the company introduced an enhanced software program called *Windows 3.0*, featuring graphical interfaces for the MS-DOS operating system. By September 1990, over 800,000 copies of the program had been shipped. Applications software produced by the company include widely acclaimed spreadsheet programs, word processors, file managers, project managers, communications programs, and graphic programs. The company also sells a large assortment of books that help customers get the most out of the programs of the company. In addition, the company sells CD-ROM products, MOUSE products, and other peripheral hardware.

The company is deeply entrenched in the microcomputer business and is not likely to be easily pushed aside by any competitors.

*Microsoft Highlights*

Recent sales: $804 million
Average sales growth 1982–1989: 65.1%
Recent net income: $171 million
Average net income growth 1980–1989: 78.2%
Net income profit margin, 5 year average: 20.0%
Recent long-term debt as percentage of capital: 0%
Recent return on equity: 36.1%

An 8 year investment in the stock of Microsoft Corporation rewarded investors with a 59.7% rate of return.

## Minnesota Mining & Manufacturing Company (3M)

3M is a highly diversified company centered on innovative research and new product development. One of the top goals of the company is to derive 25% of annual sales from new products that have been introduced during the last 5 years. Compensation and bonuses for key management personnel are closely tied to the amount of sales that are derived each year from innovative new product introductions.

The industrial sector of the company produces pressure-sensitive tapes, coated abrasives, cleaning materials, roofing granules, and specialty chemicals.

Information and imaging products include computer diskettes, data cartridges, videotape, printing plates, medical diagnostic products, overhead projectors, and transparency films.

The life sciences sector of 3M markets medical, surgical, orthopedic, pharmaceutical, and dental products.

Consumer products include Scotch tapes, Post-it notes, and other office supplies.

The company is sensitive to the slow growth of the U.S. economy but 3M is setting its sights on foreign markets, where economies are healthier. The company is one of very few that publicly states specific plans for new products to fuel 25% of annual sales. Intangible asset management is a stated goal at 3M.

*3M Highlights*

Recent sales: $12 billion
Average sales growth 1980–1989: 7.8%
Recent net income: $1.2 billion
Average net income growth 1980–1989: 7.0%
Net income profit margin, 5 year average: 9.7%
Recent long-term debt as percentage of capital: 13.3%
Recent return on equity: 22.9%

A 10 year investment in the stock of 3M rewarded investors with a 19.2% rate of return.

## NIKE, Incorporated

Transformation of the lowly sneaker into $1.7 billion of athletic shoe sales is the hallmark of NIKE. In 1990 the company announced that it had become the largest sports and fitness footwear and apparel company in the world. Almost anywhere in the world the NIKE logo can be found on footwear, jogging shorts, tennis clothes, sweatshirts, ski wear, other athletic apparel, and accessory items like athletic bags. The company has exploited its technologically advanced footwear by expanding the customer awareness that different sports required specifically designed footwear. No longer do weekend sports warriors have one pair of sneakers. Closets are now filled with different shoes for different activities including basketball, running, fitness, cross-training, and racquet ball. A large percentage of sales never see the heat of competition. Very often, NIKE products are purchased for casual and leisure wear.

One of the company's most valuable assets is the NIKE trademark, which is registered in over 70 countries. The company vigorously protects its trademarks against infringement.

Exploitation of NIKE's strong market position has been accomplished by offering a line of technical performance shoes specifically designed and developed for kids. Also, the acquisition in 1988 of Cole-Haan provides a unique opportunity for NIKE to incorporate its air cushion technology into the prestigious brand products of Cole-Haan, thereby creating a new category of product offerings.

*NIKE Highlights*

Recent sales: $1.7 billion
Average sales growth 1980–1989: 22.8%
Recent net income: $167 million
Average net income growth 1980–1989: 32.8%
Net income profit margin, 5 year average: 5.8%
Recent long-term debt as percentage of capital: 5.7%
Recent return on equity: 34.2%

A 10 year investment in the stock of NIKE rewarded investors with a 46.1% rate of return.

## Philip Morris Companies

Philip Morris is the world's largest consumer packaged goods company. Products include cigarettes (Marlboro), beverages (Miller Beer), and the food products of General Foods and Kraft. The intangible assets of the company are represented by one of the greatest trademark portfolios in the world. Included are Marlboro, Benson & Hedges, Merit, Virginia Slims, Maxwell House, Yuban, Sanka, Brim, Post, Jell-O, Log Cabin, Bird's Eye, Kool-Aid, Oscar Meyer, Kraft, Velveeta, Miracle Whip, Sealtest, Miller High Life, Miller Lite, and Lowenbrau.

In the mature markets of Philip Morris, intangible asset magic is being practiced with the introduction of new products that extend well known trademarks. Jell-O has introduced ready-to-eat puddings and frozen pudding pops. Kool-Aid is being extended with a line of ready-to-drink single-serving products.

The company has extraordinary cash flow from cigarette operations and is continually seeking trademarked product acquisitions to expand its line of brands.

In 1989 the company spent well over $2 billion in advertising as support for its most important intangible assets.

*Philip Morris Highlights*

Recent sales: $49.5 billion
Average sales growth 1980–1989: 17.6%

Recent net income: $3.6 billion
Average net income growth 1980–1989: 22.5%
Net income profit margin, 5 year average: 6.5%
Recent long-term debt as percentage of capital: 59.6%
Recent return on equity: 31.3%

A 10 year investment in the stock of Philip Morris rewarded investors with a 41.7% rate of return.

## Procter & Gamble Company

Procter & Gamble is a leading manufacturer of household and personal care products based on a combination of innovative research and the promotion of illustrious trademarks. Some of the trademarks include Tide, Crest, Spic and Span, Citrus Hill, Oil of Olay, and Vicks NyQuil. Research spending for 1989 amounted to $628 million.

One of the most valuable intangible assets aside from the portfolio of trademarks is the distribution network of the company. It has exploited this great asset by acquiring new products to put into the pipeline. The company acquired the Old Spice line of products from American Cyanamid and also acquired all of Noxell. In addition, the company has formed an alliance with Rorer to market over-the-counter drugs, while Rorer will focus on the development of P&G gastrointestinal products.

*Procter & Gamble Highlights*

Recent sales: $21.4 billion
Average sales growth 1980–1989: 7.9%
Recent net income: $1.2 billion
Average net income growth 1980–1989: 7.2%
Net income profit margin, 5 year average: 4.4%
Recent long-term debt as percentage of capital: 32.9%
Recent return on equity: 21.1%

A 10 year investment in the stock of Procter & Gamble rewarded investors with a 25.8% rate of return.

## Summary

The rewards of investing in some of the world's best intangible asset companies are presented in Exhibit 11-1.

These aren't the only great intangible asset companies. Others can be found by looking for companies that have trademarks, technological expertise, copyrights, distribution, networks, and other intangibles.

Check to see that proper care and feeding are provided in the form of continued research or advertising.

Give special attention to companies that are pursuing thoughtful exploitation strategies like licensing, expansion exploitation, and joint ventures.

Follow diligent fundamental analysis with careful intangible asset analysis. Understand that the sources of earnings and growth are the intangible assets of companies.

This book has focused on the power of intangible assets: the power to command markets, obtain premium prices, manufacture superior profits, create competitive barriers, and fuel growth. Coming back to George Gilder: "Today, the ascendant nations and corporations are masters not of land and material resources but of ideas and technologies."

*Exhibit 11-1*    Stock Returns from Ten of the Best

| Ticker | Exchange | Company | 10 Year Return (%) | 5 Year Return (%) |
|--------|----------|---------|--------------------|--------------------|
| DIS | | Disney | 24.6 | 35.8 |
| HNZ | | Heinz | 27.8 | 21.9 |
| JNJ | | Johnson & Johnson | 20.0 | 26.0 |
| LOC | | Loctite | 13.8 | 29.8 |
| MRK | | Merck | 23.5 | 37.0 |
| MSFT | | Microsoft[a] | N A | 59.7 |
| MMM | | 3M | 14.8 | 19.2 |
| MO | | Philip Morris | 28.9 | 41.7 |
| NIKE | | NIKE | N A | 46.1 |
| PG | | Procter & Gamble | 19.3 | 25.8 |
| DJ30 | | Dow Jones Average | 10.6 | 14.4 |
| SP400 | | Standard & Poors | 14.4 | 16.4 |

[a] Note that Microsoft data reflect that the company has been traded publicly for less than 5 years.

## Reference Books on Fundamental Analysis

*Competitive Strategies: Techniques for Analyzing Industries and Competitors*, by Michael E. Porter, Free Press, New York, 1980.

*Fundamental Analysis: A Back-to-Basics Investment Guide to Selecting Quality Stocks*, by John C. Ritchie, Jr., Probus Publishing Company, Chicago, Illinois, 1989.

*Security Analysis: Principles and Techniques*, 4th edition, by Benjamin Graham, David L. Dodd, and Sidney Cottle, McGraw-Hill Book Company, New York, 1962.

*The Intelligent Investor*, 4th revised edition, by Benjamin Graham, Harper & Row, New York, 1973.

*The New Stock Market: A Complete Guide to the Latest Research, Analysis and Performance*, by Diana R. Harrington, Frank J. Fabozzi, and H. Russell Fogler, Probus Publishing Company, Chicago, Illinois, 1990.

# Appendix

# INTANGIBLE ASSET CHECKLIST

When performing fundamental analysis on a company, the investigation should focus on identifying the existence of intangible assets because, as discussed throughout this book, these are the true source of premium pricing, market dominance, superior profits, and overall growth. In this appendix a list of specific intangible assets are identified with a brief description provided for each.

The search for intangible assets should include all aspects of the company. They exist at all levels of company operations including sales activities, marketing programs, distribution procedures, administrative operations, research programs, employee relations, financial arrangements, manufacturing procedures, and raw material supplies.

## Intangible Asset Checklist

Assembled work force
Backlog
Captive parts annuity
Computer software
Copyrights
Core deposits
Customer lists
Distribution networks
Distribution rights
Favorable contracts
Joint ventures
Licensing agreements
Loan portfolios
Mortgage servicing rights
Patents
Regulatory approvals
Satellite Transponder Leases
Technological know-how
Television and radio spots
Trademarks
Vendor lists

*Assembled Work Force*   In many businesses the presence of a skilled work force that is knowledgeable about company procedures and possesses expertise in certain fields is vital to continued profitability and growth. Some industries require skilled craftspeople such as machine tool operators, while others require scientific expertise that in some cases is available only among a rare number of individuals. When a skilled work force is important to a business, a diligent fundamental analysis should be made to ascertain the types of salary, benefits, and other personnel policies in existence for maintaining key personnel in place. In high-tech industries research personnel possessing rare skills and knowledge can be the keystone to the ultimate success of the business.

*Backlog*    Many businesses such as construction businesses and capital equipment manufacturers have a backlog of orders. This represents future earnings from sales that have already been closed. A company with a strong backlog has, at least on a limited basis, a guarantee of future profitability.

A backlog that is declining may indicate that something is wrong within the company. Product characteristics may be less desirable than new competitor offerings or the company may be falling behind in areas such as customer service. A falling backlog can be a sign that other intangible assets of the company have been weakened. A rising backlog can indicate that the products and services of the company are gaining in popularity and market penetration.

*Captive Parts Annuity*    The continued purchase of replacement parts for capital equipment that has already been sold to customers can be an extraordinarily profitable portion of a business. If a company manufactures and sells complex capital equipment like aircraft, defense equipment, computer equipment, and other items requiring a substantial customer investment, then the customer purchasing the original item must continually return to the manufacturer for replacement parts and accessories. Typically, these items are sold at healthy premium prices, contributing healthy profit margins. Premium pricing of these parts reflects the near monopoly position that the original equipment manufacturer possesses as the only source for these parts.

The term *captive* is used to describe the nature of the relationship with the customers. Once the original equipment is purchased, few options exist as sources for spare and replacement parts. The term *annuity* refers to the regularity of receiving orders. The continued receipt of orders is a function of the life of the original equipment and the age of the equipment that the company has placed with its customers.

In some businesses the original piece of equipment is sold at an extremely low level of profit or at break-even in order to capture the monopoly position for regular maintenance and accessory parts.

The sale of spare parts, replacement parts, and accessories can be a substantial portion of a business. Some companies can estimate the amount of sales from this component of the business very accurately and therefore plan ahead to achieve the greatest amount of profitability. Sales of new equipment may be hurt during economic downturns but replacement parts are usually very resilient.

*Computer Software*    Valuable computer software can be related to a company product or can represent internal controls that enhance the efficiency of operations. Lotus Development Corp. has computer products like *Lotus 1-2-3* that serve as the foundation of their business. Federal Express has internal software and procedures that allow customers to ascertain the location of shipments in less than an hour. Federal Express uses this software to control operations and also as a strong selling point to differentiate it from competitors.

Computer software is currently protected under copyright laws, which only protect the expression of an idea and not the idea itself. Aggressive competition in all areas of product software abound, including programs for spreadsheet, accounting systems, word processing, database management, and utilities. The remaining economic life during which economic benefits are derived is shorter for product line software because of constant competitor improvements. Software associated with internal controls generally have a much longer useful life.

*Copyrights*    As previously discussed, these legally protected "expressions of an idea" include films, books, articles, software, television programs, and other works. Decades of repeat sales are often possible with exclusive rights retained by the owner. A portfolio of classic copyrighted material can have decades of profit potential. Other copyrighted items are associated with fads that quickly lose consumer appeal. When assessing an investment that is based on copyrights it is important to determine the longevity of the material. Also important is the existence of a development program designed to create new materials to replace fading items.

*Core Deposits*    In banking, one of the major assets that contributes to value is a stable base of depositors that maintain accounts of various kinds with the bank such as checking accounts and savings accounts. The amount of deposits represents the foundation of a bank and serves as the basis on which an earnings spread can be collected representing the difference between the amount at which the bank makes loans and the amount of interest that the bank pays to depositors.

Core deposits have definite remaining lives. Deposits are removed from banks for many reasons, including relocation of residence, financing college educations, purchasing new homes, and investment in other types of securities. When analyzing the stability of core deposits, the means for replacing lost accounts should be investigated.

*Customer Lists*   A list of established customer relationships comprised of individuals that repeatedly order from the company can have extraordinary value. The information contained in such lists usually includes the preferences of the customer, the buying patterns of the customer, and the history of purchases that have been received from the customer. In a sense, a list of loyal customers that regularly provide the company with sales is similar to the captive parts and annuity.

*Distribution Networks*   Many manufacturing companies do not possess an extensive staff of sales individuals. Instead, a network of independent distributors are used to find customers and get orders. These distributors receive a commission on each sale. They also can be a vital source of customer information. Many product enhancement ideas have come from customers through comments made to representatives of the distributor. Development of a distribution network can require an extensive amount of time as prospective distributors are identified, interviewed, qualified, and educated about the products that they will carry. Without a well established distribution network, even the very best products cannot generate sales and profits.

*Distribution Rights*   A contract or agreement that provides exclusive rights to distribute a successful product can be extremely valuable even when the product itself is not owned. Similar profit potential, as associated with owning the product, is presented to a company that has exclusive marketing rights or distribution rights. While this type of agreement might not be as valuable as owning the product outright, it has a significant value depending on the underlying economic characteristics of the distributed product.

Distributors focus their skills on selling. Rights to represent a product to their customer base expand their business and profit opportunities. Distribution rights are usually defined in legal agreements which possess termination dates. Many renew on a regular basis, with distribution rights lasting for decades. Some distributors can lose these rights, however, if minimum amounts of orders are not met or if the manufacturer of the product changes marketing strategies and decides to establish its own sales force.

*Favorable Contracts*   Earnings can be enhanced for a company when it has favorable costs associated with contracts that provide it with services or supplies. It is important to remember when studying this intangible asset that the most favorable contracts have termination dates at which the advantageous pricing may not be renewed.

Favorable contracts can exist for companies in the following areas:

Distribution agreements
Employment contracts
Financing arrangements with banks
Insurance premiums
Rental rates for office facilities
Rental rates for manufacturing facilities
Raw material supplies
Professional services
Utility contracts with advantageous pricing

*Joint Ventures*   Business ventures where unique intangible assets are pooled under one roof allow optimal exploitation of these assets. Joint ventures allow companies to gain access to other intangible assets that they cannot reproduce for themselves. This business strategy is gaining in popularity among some of the largest companies in the world like Merck, Johnson & Johnson, and Du Pont. Chapter 8 fully discusses the many benefits of joint ventures.

*License Agreements*   This intangible asset was also discussed in great detail in Chapter 8 as another business strategy for full exploitation of intangibles. It involves valuable rights that are transferred when a company gains the right to manufacture and sell another party's product. Possessing a license agreement can propel the sales and earnings growth of a company. From the point of view of a licenser, the agreement can serve as a continuing stream of royalty payments that can be gained without great effort on the part of the licenser. Texas Instruments derives more net profit from license royalties than from operating its own business.

*Loan Portfolios*   In banking, core deposits were identified as a valuable foundation of the business. The other side of the equation is the collection of loans that the bank makes to businesses and individuals. A portfolio of quality loans is indeed valuable when a positive spread exists between the amount of interest paid to depositors and the amount of interest earned on loans. Quality portfolios are also becoming rare in the present economic downturn.

*Mortgage Servicing Rights*   Some companies make money by servicing mortgages. The companies do not own the mortgages nor do they have any rights with regard to the underlying real estate. These companies possess contracts that require them to collect mortgage payments and disburse them to the proper lenders. For this service a mortgage servicing company receives a fee that is based on the amount of mortgages being serviced. Other examples of this type of business are companies that collect and disperse the funds associated with credit card transactions.

*Patents*   Temporary and exclusive monopolies are legally conveyed to inventors for 17 years in exchange for publicly disclosing the secrets of the new invention. Patents cover designs, products, manufacturing techniques, plants, and even animals. A patent holder has the right to exclude all others from using the invention during the life of the patent. This allows the patent owner to price products that are associated with the patented invention at whatever the market will bear. Competitive pricing pressures from "me-too" products are absent during the protection period. Consequently, superior profits can be associated with ownership of patents. Commercial success is not *guaranteed* with the issuance of a patent, just the right to pursue commercialization exclusively.

Instant photography patents that are held by Polaroid have allowed the company to become the only game in town when it comes to selling instant cameras. In 1990 Kodak had to pay $1 billion to Polaroid for infringing on its patent rights. Texas Instruments receives approximately $150 million per year from licensing

...ented technology to others. Xerox Corp. was founded on copier technology patents.

*Regulatory Approvals*   In many industries a vital component of operations is obtaining and maintaining certain licenses and approvals that are granted by government regulatory agencies. A patented drug product, for example, cannot be marketed regardless of its health benefits until the FDA approves the drug. Airline routes are allocated by the government and utility rates are approved by local commissions. Costs associated with gaining such approval can be extensive. In the case of drug approvals, the testing required to gain FDA approval can sometimes approach $100 million.

*Satellite Transponder Leases*   Many companies offer services that use satellite communications requiring access to satellites. Transponders that are being used by these companies are typically not owned by the company but are leased from other companies that own satellites. As more of these services are offered, access to transponders can become a coveted intangible asset.

*Technological Know-how*   Understanding what works and does not work is extraordinarily valuable. Decades of research success and failure define the research and manufacturing techniques that a company uses. Technological know-how can involve unpatented and patented products or processes. It can also be as simple as knowing the proper heat setting for mass producing crispy cookies at Procter & Gamble.

*Television and Radio Spots*   Some companies perform a great deal of regular advertising. As with anything else, there are economies of scale that can be enjoyed by buying large amounts of television and radio time slots.

*Trademarks*   Chapter 5 discusses the powerful intangible asset of trademarks in great detail. Trademarks can dominate markets, achieve premium pricing, generate superior profits, and serve as the foundation for new product lines. Consumer perceptions are sometimes the only strength of a trademark, but possessing such a characteristic can carry extraordinary value. Trademarks mean status (Rolex), safety (Volvo), reliability (Maytag), and sex appeal (Chanel).

*Vendor Lists*   A collection of information about suppliers can be crucial to the continuing success of distributors and mail order companies. A reliable source of unique and quality products is as important as the customer list. The data typically found in this valuable vendor list include information about pricing, terms, product offerings, key personnel, support services offered, and product quality.

# INDEX